There is good food. Lots of good food. Great food? There ain't much great food around. There are distinct reasons why some food is only just good and some food is just plain great. Umami and the Maillard reaction are two reasons why a dish will make the leap from good to great.

Most of the better cooks we meet can make a couple of great dishes. But if you ask them what makes that dish great, they are hard-pressed to say exactly what they do that makes the difference between good and great. They just know that one dish is only okay and another dish is great. This one works, but that great one sells like, well, hotcakes.

Great food has a lifelong learning curve.

Umami and the Maillard reaction are essential factors to understand if you want to know why some of your soups, sauces, and other dishes achieve greatness. Understanding these two items alone will help to enhance all your dishes.

It is for each of us to try to understand the reasons for that great background taste, that perfect texture—the color and aroma that make people hungry. Little nuances of flavor, technique, and ingredients make huge differences in the final product.

MAKING
GOOD
FOOD
GREAT

MAKING GOOD FOOD GREAT

UMAMI AND THE MAILLARD REACTION

John Griffin and Jeff Gold

MAKING GOOD FOOD GREAT
UMAMI AND THE MAILLARD REACTION

iUniverse books may be ordered through booksellers or by contacting:

iUniverse
1663 Liberty Drive
Bloomington, IN 47403
www.iuniverse.com
1-800-Authors (1-800-288-4677)

Because of the dynamic nature of the Internet, any web addresses or links contained in this book may have changed since publication and may no longer be valid. The views expressed in this work are solely those of the author and do not necessarily reflect the views of the publisher, and the publisher hereby disclaims any responsibility for them.

Any people depicted in stock imagery provided by Thinkstock are models,
and such images are being used for illustrative purposes only.
Certain stock imagery © Thinkstock.

ISBN: 978-1-5320-2498-6 (sc)
ISBN: 978-1-5320-2497-9 (e)

Library of Congress Control Number: 2017910694

Print information available on the last page.

iUniverse rev. date: 08/18/2017

For Suzy

Simply adding good flavors to a dish is not enough. If this is your style, you will be making dishes that are *delicate*. This is another word for *tasteless*

INTRODUCTION

Making great food is difficult to describe. Most chefs will know great food when they taste it, will know great food when they make it, but will have a hard time being specific in why this dish is great, and that dish just good.

There are a few names and phrases that are familiar to the experienced chef. Names such as Umami and the Maillard Reaction are known to most folks, but they are not really understood. These two concepts are the key to turning good food into great food.

Umami, "the fifth taste", is a defined flavor, with taste receptors on your palate, and a gigantic contributor to great food. The Maillard Reaction, "the browning effect", is a well-known but little understood phenomenon. The word "caramelization" is used frequently on menus, and is more commercially acceptable than "Maillard". The confusion is understandable in terms of menus, but it needs to be understood in terms of method.

Many cooks and many businesses make a big deal out of "plating." Their dishes are constructed in beautiful, elegant, and surprising ways that are vastly pleasing to the eye. This is great presentation, and it is an important piece of serving meals. But beautiful food is easy to make. It is not great food. Great food has to *taste* great.

Most commercial products are packed with salt, sugar, and fat. Of course they taste good. Pack anything with salt, sugar, and fat, and it'll taste good. You'll want seconds. These foods are not good for you, and they are not great.

I have had great food. It is safe, it is wholesome, and it is so delicious that you don't need salt. The difference between a good dish and a great dish has to do with very small changes in ingredients and technique. Though the changes are small, the difference they make is immense.

This is a discussion of how to turn your good dish into a great dish. You don't need a new recipe, some esoteric, highly involved culinary techniques, or the finest and most unusual ingredients. You will use simple culinary basics that you already know, learn some additional useful facts, and apply them for added taste, aroma, color, and texture.

This discussion is not about plating. Anyone who has a good eye can take ordinary everyday plain food and make it into a beautiful plate. It still needs salt; it still is only good food. It just looks great. I want food that looks *and* tastes great, can be made great again and again, and is good for me.

The great cooks of the world have little nuances of technique that change an original recipe from good to great. Those little nuances are very important, and mainly involve umami and the Maillard reaction. We will discuss a few additional points that are important. These include ingredients, ratios, recipes, reductions, and combinations.

Ratios are important. Too much celery in a dish, and it becomes a celery dish. Too much cumin, and it just tastes bad. Add the right amount of either, and the dish is delicious. This applies to everything you make. Just as baking is considered both a science and an art, all cooking should be considered a blend of ratios, ingredients, and techniques. Get them all right at the right time, and your dish is great.

Learning how to work with Umami, the Maillard Reaction, and a few other simple concepts can change good food into great food. This book is a brief exploration of these basic cooking concepts, hoping to add a few good tastes into your recipes. We hope you enjoy our work.

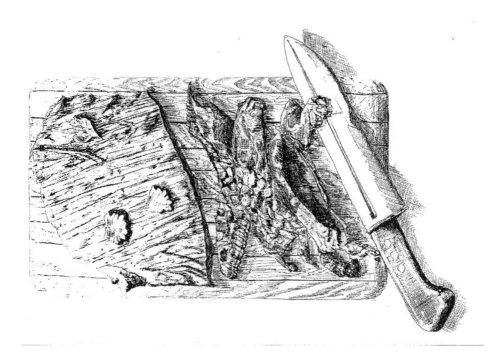

CONTENTS

Introduction xi

Chapter 1:   Some Definitions 1
Chapter 2:   Food Safety 13
Chapter 3:   Making Good Food Great 23
Chapter 4:   What Goes Into Great Food 36
Chapter 5:   The Rubber Chicken Dinner 48
Chapter 6:   The Maillard Reaction 52
Chapter 7:   Introducing Umami 59
Chapter 8:   Two Cooks 63
Chapter 9:   Basic Great Food Ingredients 69
Chapter 10: Concentrating Flavors 72
Chapter 11: Ratios 74
Chapter 12: Writing Recipes 79
Chapter 13: The Most Difficult of Great Food:
            French Onion Soup and the Turkey Club 84
Chapter 14: Clean and Simple Food 91
Chapter 15: House-Made Sodas 102
Chapter 16: Making Good Food Bad 110
Chapter 17: Reducing Salt Using Umami and Maillard 117

The Final Word 125
About the Authors 129
Jeff Gold 130
Elliott Wennet 132
Index 137

CHAPTER 1

Some Definitions

good food: Food that is safe, wholesome, nutritious, and pleasing to the eye and palate, but needs salt.

great food: Food that is safe, wholesome, nutritious, and pleasing to the eye and palate, with such great flavor and aroma that very little salt is needed.

umami: Japanese term for the "fifth taste"—the first four being sweet, sour, bitter, and acid. It can be translated as "savory" or "deliciousness." Adding umami ingredients, in combination and in concentration, will lead to all ingredients having improved flavor.

the Maillard reaction: A chemical reaction between amino acids, a reducing sugar, and heat. It is demonstrated by the browning of meat, the browning of breads and baked goods, and the color of maple syrup. It increases flavor and aroma, leading to greatness. (Maillard is pronounced My-*YAR*.)

Grilled Crimini and Asparagus Salad

Makes 12 appetizer or salad servings

Crimini mushrooms, if cooked just so, will give off a delicious liquid that has many uses. I use this mushroom "sauce" as a marinade for many types of vegetables and seafood. This is perhaps simplest and best example of using the fine Umami flavor in these dark mushrooms. This may be served hot next to a prime steak, or as part of a cold salad next to a rice and lentil burger. This is a very versatile dish, which may be used for several days after preparation, on many menu items.

1 pound	Crimini Mushrooms
2 Tbs	XVOO
1 pound	Dry Red Lentils
1 pound	Fresh Asparagus
8 ounces	Roasted Red Peppers
1 Tbs	Low Sodium Soy Sauce

Wash and trim the mushrooms, and put on paper towels to dry.

Peel the asparagus bottom sections, and cut off some of the bottoms so they are all the same length. Cook the asparagus in a little water until they are just done. Put aside to cool. They should be fully cooked, but only barely so.

Wash the red lentils and cook in some water. After a pretty short time, like 5 minutes, strain the lentils out and pour them on a sheet pan to cool. Any more than 5 minutes and they're mush. You want whole slightly crunchy lentils for this salad.

In a heavy pan (I use a big Griswald, a large cast iron skillet), brown the mushrooms in a little Extra Virgin Olive Oil. Do this in a couple of stages, with very high heat. You need to keep the mushrooms from touching each other as they brown. When each batch of mushrooms has browned, put them in a large stainless bowl. Sprinkle with a little soy sauce. You should be using Tamari Sauce if you'd like to keep this gluten free.

Put all the browned mushrooms in the cooler for at least an hour, maybe overnight. They will give off a very dark liquid. When cool, cut the mushrooms in whatever shape you'd like, and return to the liquid.

In this instance, display the asparagus decoratively on a flat serving dish that will hold some liquid. Spoon some cooled lentils on the side of the asparagus. Add some sliced roasted red peppers, or another vegetable for color. Pour the mushrooms, and the liquid over the asparagus, cover, and put back in the cooler to marinate for a while. Use within a few days.

The combination of flavors, marinated in the most delicious mushroom juice, is delicious. Keep any mushrooms and juice for other delicious uses.

Eggplant Rolatini

Makes about 12 servings

Most of the Eggplant Rolatini we have been served is not great food. They are generally filled with soft cheese, and served with poor tomato sauce and unaged Mozzarella.

This recipe includes such Umami ingredients as aged cheese, freshly reduced tomatoes, aged ham and asparagus. It uses Maillard to brown the eggplant, and the cheese. This dish will also sit well in a warming oven for about an hour, in the right pan and covered well, making it an easy dish for restaurant or dinner party service.

4 each	Medium Sized Eggplants (about 4 pounds total)
	Freshly ground black pepper
4 ounces	XVOO
24 thin slices	Gruyere cheese (enough to cover the sliced eggplant)
24 thin slices	Prosciutto ham
24 each	Asparagus spears, peeled and blanched
12 each	Broccoli florets, blanched and cut small
8 ounces	Parmesan and Romano cheese
4 cups	Fresh tomato Sauce (Concasse), recipe follows

Place a rack over a large baking sheet. Cut 2 long slices from the ends of the eggplant and discard. Cut the eggplants lengthwise, into 3/8-inch thick slices. We are looking for 24 similarly sized center slices. Arrange eggplant slices onto rack. Sprinkle with sea salt to help remove excess moisture and any bitterness from the eggplants. Set aside for about 15 minutes. Rinse off the salt from the eggplants, and pat dry with a towel. This will help remove excess moisture and any bitterness from the eggplants.

Heat a heavy pan and preheat the oven to 400 degrees F. A cast iron grill pan works best, or any heavy pan so you get lots of heat. Or you may do the eggplant on a gas, charcoal, or wood grill. Grill the eggplant until lightly browned on each side and tender. Remove slices from the grill pan and allow to cool.

Place 24 perfect slices on your board. On each slice, place the slices of Gruyere cheese then top with the thin sliced Prosciutto ham. Add some broccoli. Halve the asparagus. Place 2- 4 inch pieces (base and top) on the wider end of the eggplant slices. From that end, roll the eggplant.

Place the eggplant rollatini into a greased baking dish, seam side down. Continue with remaining eggplant. Sprinkle liberally with Parmesan and Romano cheeses. Place a small amount of the tomato sauce on top of the eggplant rollatini. Bake or broil until browned on top. Place 2 rolls on each plate and place a liberal amount of sauce covering ½ of the rolls. Sprinkle with more cheese and serve.

Concasse

Makes about 10 cups of sauce

This is a great base for all sorts of tomato sauces. It is gently cooked, fresh, and lightly reduced. You may add all sorts of flavors to this sauce, by sautéing some shallots, garlic, dry sausage, fresh basil, oregano, or any flavor you'd like. Do not overdo the flavorings, as the fresh tomato flavor is what you are looking for.

Tomato Concasse may be kept in the cooler for several days, and added to lots of recipes, either as a main flavoring, or a simple Umami addition to a frittata, soup, or sauce. It is a great addition to any omelet.

At home we freeze our tomatoes fresh from the garden. Simply dip in boiling water, peel, trim, juice, and stick in sealable bags. This is a great source for fresh tomato concasse all winter long.

4 pounds	Fresh very ripe Plum Tomatoes (or)
4 cans	Diced tomatoes, drained
(It is important to get a top quality tomato for yield, consistency, and natural flavor.)	
4 ounces	Extra-virgin olive oil
8 ounces	Fresh shallots, peeled and diced
1 knob	Fresh garlic, peeled and chopped cloves
Freshly ground black pepper	
8 ounces	Chopped Italian parsley
1 stick	Unsalted butter, optional

Dip each fresh tomato in boiling water for about 10 seconds, and cool quickly, under running water, or on ice. The peels will now come off easily. Cut out any green or bad spots. Cut the tomatoes in half and squeeze out the juice. Put the tomato meat in a strainer to drain. Or, drain the canned tomatoes and reserve the juice.

Chop the peeled and juiced tomatoes coarsely.

In a large casserole heat the oil. Add onion and garlic and sweat until soft and translucent. Add drained tomatoes and simmer uncovered until they are just hot. Add some tomato juice to desired consistency. Add chopped parsley. If sauce still tastes acidic, add unsalted butter, 1 tablespoon at a time to round out the flavors. Serve when ready. The tomatoes in the sauce should be only warmed thoroughly when using canned. If using fresh tomatoes, cook no more that 3-5 minutes only, just enough to soften.

If not using all the sauce, allow it to cool completely and pour 1 to 2 cup portions into freezer plastic bags. Keep in the cooler for up to 7 day, or freeze for up to 6 months.

Rack of Lamb with Strawberry and Garlic Sauce

Makes 4 servings

Strawberry and garlic sauce tastes like neither. It is an example of two Umami ingredients combining to form a third very different and very interesting taste. This sauce is equally good on any grilled meat or poultry, especially London Broil, Duck Breast, or Pork Chops.

2 each	Lamb Racks
2 ounce	Bread crumbs
1 ounce	Olive oil
6 ounces	Garlic, chopped
	(it is important to use fresh garlic, not chopped in oil or water)
4 ounces	Shallots, diced
1 pound	Fresh Strawberries
1 ounce	Strawberry Jam
1 ounce	Dry Sherry
1 pint	Demi-Glace or good, thin brown sauce
1 dash	Soy Sauce

Trim the lamb and season very lightly. French the ribs. Dust the meat portion with some bread crumbs, and pat on lightly. Cover the exposed rib bones with aluminum foil and keep aside until ready to roast.

Sweat the shallots and garlic in a little olive oil for at least 5 minutes. Allow them to brown just a little. Trim the strawberries, and reserve about 4 ounces for garnish. Put the rest of them in the pan with the onions and garlic, and cook down slowly until it is a good paste. Add a little jam at the end of this time. Deglaze the pan with a little Sherry, and bring to a boil. Add the brown sauce, bring to a boil, and allow to simmer for at least 15 minutes. This sauce should be rather thin, rather than thick.

Strain this sauce very well, so that no bits of onion or garlic remain, and bring to a boil. Trim and dice the remaining strawberries, and add to the boiling sauce. Add just a little soy sauce, and keep warm.

Roast the lamb by placing in a very hot oven, like 450º or higher. Turn the oven right down to less than 300º, and roast until it is rare. It will keep cooking when removed from the oven, so pull it a little early. Allow to sit for at least 5 minutes before cutting.

At service, slice the lamb into chops, and serve two to each guest. Serve the thin sauce boiling hot under the lamb, with a little on the bone (take off the foil).

CHAPTER 2

Food Safety

No discussion about food can start without a word about serving safe meals. The greatest dish anyone's every made—with the finest taste, garnish, and eye appeal—that gets you sick is not great food. It is not good food.

Food safety is generally misunderstood. There are a few diseases, food-borne illnesses, and toxins that may develop in food and make you sick in a short time. But, for the most part, dangerous food-borne illnesses take many days or many weeks to develop after you have been exposed. Good old salmonella and E. coli may be in your system for over a month before you start getting symptoms. Those symptoms can kill you.

The first part of food safety starts with where you get your food. Do you trust the store or deliveryman to bring you food that is wholesome? Have the products been kept at the proper temperature? Is there reason to suspect tampering with your products? If you start with safe food, you have a chance of serving safe food.

Bacteria and viruses are the main culprits in food-borne illness outbreaks. Yes, there are other problems possible, but understanding bacteria and viruses in terms of the food you make, store, and reheat will go a long way in helping to serve good food. Bacteria will grow in food. Viruses will be transported by food. Bacteria will be killed by some heat and viruses by a lot of heat.

The best way to stop the growth of bacteria is to keep your food products out of the "danger zone"—40 to 140 degrees—and keep food for only a few days. Old food that has been temperature compromised is potentially dangerous food. You can't see, smell, or taste bacteria. They're just there.

The best way to prevent viruses from contaminating your food is to wash your hands. Use clean equipment and sanitize your surfaces. Gloves only help a little, as dirty gloves are as bad as dirty hands. Wash your hands.

If you can be pretty certain that the food you are serving is safe, you may go on to the next chapter and look into making your food taste a little better.

Meanwhile, as appearance is a major part of any menu, I will touch on kitchen cleanliness—at least in the basic areas that will make a dramatic difference in how your guests judge your dishes. A clean kitchen does not mean the food is safe, but the two areas are related. I can say by experience that a dirty kitchen generally serves food that I would not want to eat. In a commercial kitchen, it is imperative that the cleaning be done when there is no food being served, as you need to thoroughly clean with serious chemicals that cannot be used around food. It costs a lot of money to clean a kitchen.

Food safety rules for home and work include the following:

- Wash your hands.
- Use only cleaned and sanitized cutting boards, knives, and equipment.
- Beware of sponges and towels that harbor pathogens. Use paper towels.
- Keep food either cold or hot, under 40 degrees or over 140 degrees.
- Store raw meats and fish on the bottom shelf, in pans so they don't drip.
- If in doubt, throw it out.
- Wash your hands.

Anadama Bread

This bread has a long history. It is a recipe hundreds of years old, and has never been out of style. My first view of this bread came from the James Beard book, <u>Beard On Bread</u>. Anna dropped a loaf, that's how he says it got its name. This particular book is a great addition to any culinary library. It is a masterpiece in format and information.

Makes 6 loaves of bread, or about 60 rolls

1 oz	Dry Yeast
4 oz	Sugar
5 cups	Warm Water
6 oz	Butter
12 oz	Molasses
1 oz	Salt
1 pound	Yellow Cornmeal
2 pounds	Bread Flour
2 pounds	Whole Wheat Flour

Dissolve the dry yeast on ¼ cup of warm, not hot, water, and allow to sit for 5 minutes. Add the sugar, and the rest of the water, and mix well. Heat the molasses, the butter, and the salt together, in a small saucepan, to lukewarm, and add to the yeast mixture. Add the cornmeal, and mix well. Add the flour, 1 cup at a time, mixing well with a spoon until it gets too thick for a spoon. You may need more or less flour depending on your flour and the weather. The dough should be soft. When the flour is incorporated, turn onto a lightly floured board. Knead the dough for about 5 minutes, until it becomes strong.

Cover the dough, and allow to sit for about an hour, depending on the temperature of the room. It will get about double in size. When this happens, press the dough down, stretch it out a little, and roll it into a large ball. This you cut into loaf sized pieces, or roll sized pieces.

Lightly grease six loaf pans, or place free form as loaves or rolls on sheet pans with parchment paper. Place the dough pieces in the pans, and cover with a dry cloth. Allow to rise to where it is almost to the top of the pan. This dough can also be made free form, without a bread pan.

Preheat the oven to 425°. Cut the top of the breads for decoration, and brush with little bit of water. Place the breads in the oven, and in 10 minutes, lower the heat to 325°. The breads will be done about 35 minutes after that. Test by picking up the pan with a cloth, and turning the bread out onto your hand.

Tap it on the bottom and it'll sound hollow, or go back in the oven for a few more minutes. Allow to cool for at least an hour before you cut it. This bread will improve with a day or more after it is baked.

Biscochas

Makes about 100 cookies

Every family has its favorite foods. Some families are blessed with recipes that have lasted for generations. Holiday time is when these foods come out. The origins of certain foods are lost to the ages, but the recipes and methods have been passed down to the present day. The family member who takes it onto his or herself to make these family traditional recipes each year really should write down the recipe and method, to ensure the continuation of the tradition, and to maybe share with the rest of the world.

This recipe has gone through a few generations, but all agree that the cookie remains the same. At Thanksgiving, Chanukah, and other times, there would be certain foods expected, among them lots and lots of Biscochas, and Challah bread. Each family member gets a big bag of cookies to bring home. The phone calls start weeks before the holiday making sure that the source would be ready with the goods.

Biscochas are a pretty simple cookie to make. A good baker can make double the following recipe in about 2 hours, and come up with 200 cookies. They last a very long time; in fact I think they improve with a week or so of age.

6 each	Eggs
1 ½ cups	Sugar
2 Tbs	Water
½ cup	Vegetable Oil
1 tsp	Pure Vanilla Extract
5 ½ cups	Flour
1 ½ tsp	Baking powder
Pinch	Salt
½ cup	Sesame seeds

Mix eggs with sugar and water, add the oil and vanilla. Sift the baking powder and salt into the flour to keep out any baking powder lumps, and add to the dough. Mix about 2 minutes, until well incorporated, but do not over mix.

Let the dough rest for about 10 minutes. Take out about half the dough, on a lightly floured cutting board. Roll into a log around 2" wide. Cut into 1" sections. Roll out each section on the board to about 3" strips, until all sections have been rolled out. Score the strips lengthwise down the middle, and then make many little slits on one side of the roll. Form into round cookies, pressing the ends together, still on the board. The cookies should look like bagels with a slit on the top, and cuts around the outside edge.

Pick up gently and place on a sheet pan with parchment paper. Wash the tops of the cookies with well-beaten eggs, lightly. Sprinkle sesame seeds on some of the cookies. Bake at 350 degrees for about 10 minutes, until they are nicely browned. Allow to cool on the pan, and place in a tin or bags. These will keep over a month in a dry tin with no refrigeration.

Challah

Challah bread looks to be daunting to the home baker, and it is a special bread. In reality, it is a very simple procedure, if you are careful and follow a few rules. Make sure the yeast and water mix is at the right temperature, not too hot or too cold. Mix well to build up the gluten in the dough. Allow the dough to rise double, form into loaves, and let rise again. Wash and bake.

Challah bread makes by far the best French toast in the world. Raisin Challah bread make the best regular toast. These loaves improve with age, and are much better a day or two old, and great from the freezer. Take a fresh loaf, several hours old, slice it, bag it, and freeze it, and you're set for breakfasts for the week.

2 cups, 4 ounces	Water
¾ ounce	Dry Yeast
2 ounces	Sugar
2 ½ pounds	Bread flour
1 ounce	Salt
Oil	2 oz
Egg yolks	3 each
Whole egg	1 each

Mix the yeast in water warmed to about 100 degrees, and half the sugar. Let sit until it starts to bubble a little. Add the rest of the ingredients, and mix well with a dough hook about 8 minutes. Cover with a damp cloth, and let sit at room temperature about an hour, until it doubles in bulk.

Cut into 4 equal portions, and shape as you wish, either rounded, straight bread, or braided. You may even make these as dinner rolls. Place on sheet pans with parchment paper. Let rest after forming, for over a half hour. Wash the tops with some beaten eggs. Bake 375 degrees for about 40 minutes.

If you are more adventurous, you may want to shape the Challah loaves in the traditional braid. This is a little different than most breads, and the resultant shape, high and tall at the top, tapered at each end, is actually a method of obtaining the most color, flavor and aroma from this rich bread dough.

The classic and most difficult braid is the six braided loaf, and this is the classic Challah loaf. It is something which you need to see first, and then practice a couple of times before you'll get it. It is worth the effort.

CHAPTER 3

Making Good Food Great

Any good food can be made great—not by adding salt or a ton of sugar, but by adhering to the following simple rules:

- *Serve safe food.* Safe food is primary. Everything else pales in comparison.
- *Use fresh ingredients and store them correctly.* Quality ingredients, stored in the right way, make for much better products. For instance, tomatoes stored at 58 degrees will be sweet; stored at 38 degrees, they will be starch. Bread is never to be stored in the refrigerator, or the starches will recrystallize and the bread will become very stale very quickly. Limes "stay alive at 55." At 35 degrees, they shrivel and dry.
- *Use umami ingredients.* Knowing umami and using reductions to concentrate umami flavors results in a greatly improved product.
- *Concentrate your flavors.* Splashing some wine in a sauce will add a little flavor. Reducing that wine with some shallots will change the sauce.
- *Understand your ratios.* Being judicious about your ingredient ratios is very important. A little diced red pepper will enhance a sauce; a lot of diced red pepper will make it into a red pepper sauce
- *Brown for flavor.* Using the Maillard reaction to brown food—adding flavor, aroma, and color—drastically changes food products for the better.
- *Serve what you know.* Serving what you know is a key element in any menu. "Muscle memory" is important. When you've done a dish a hundred times correctly, you will be able to pull it off without a hitch. You don't know a dish or its flavors until you have practiced that meal dozens or hundreds of times, made mistakes, and learned how to do the dish perfectly again and again. Now you can make this dish consistently and perfectly on any occasion.

If you were to ask good cooks who make a great soup just how they make that soup, they may have a difficult time describing exactly what they do. If those cooks understand umami, Maillard, and a few simple rules, they'll be more able to describe those little differences between good and great. This is an important part of learning to write a recipe.

Our recipes are written "cook to cook." We expect you to know the lingo and not need every single method explained over and over. Every single ingredient does not have to be perfectly weighed; the ratio is more important than a single ingredient amount.

As a simple way to describe two different recipes, we have chosen French onion soup and the turkey club sandwich. For many different reasons, we think these two dishes are the most difficult to make great. They are easy to make good, which is why they are on most menus in some way or another. But great French onion soup or a great turkey club are extremely rare—as are most great dishes. If you can learn to make great onion soup consistently, then you may enhance all items on the menu.

Miso Soup

Makes about 12 servings

I spoke with James Liu, who owns Osaka Restaurants, in Tivoli, and Rhinebeck, NY, about Miso Soup. James was amazed that I would want the recipe as he said "This is about the simplest food there is". This would be like asking your Mom for the recipe to Peanut Butter and Jelly sandwiches. I persisted, and he relented, offering us the ability to know what goes into this most healthful of soups.

Miso is a fermented soy bean curd. A prime Umami ingredient. As such, it is one of the more healthful food items available, with complete simple proteins. To make miso soup, you pretty much make a broth from this soy based product, flavor it, and garnish it. The result should be called "Japanese Penicillin", as it warms and nourishes. The ingredients are unusual to the American cook, but may easily be obtained in most health food shops.

2 ounces	Kombu seaweed
One half gallon	Water
4 ounces	Shiro (white) miso
2 ounces	Wakame seaweed
2 ounces	Tofu fresh, diced
2 each	Scallion, sliced

Cook the Kombu Seaweed in water for about 15 minutes, simmer only. Whip the Shiro Miso into the simmering water. Bring to one boil, and turn off

In a separate bowl, cover the Wakame Seaweed with cold water, and soak for 5 minutes or so. Pour off the water when well hydrated.

For each guest, place some of the Wakame Seaweed in a bowl, some diced tofu, and some sliced scallions. Pour the hot miso broth on the vegetables, and serve.

As variations, you may pour the broth over cooked soba noodles, or any noodle. You may also add any steamed vegetables, with or without the noodles.

Indian Pudding

Makes about 24 servings

Indian Pudding is a classic New England dish, a Colonial update of the Old World "Hasty Pudding". A misnomer in this case, as this recipe requires a few hours in a slow oven. The Colonials added molasses and corn meal, both much more available to them. The high molasses content makes this an especially nutritious dish. This dish should be kept hot in a food warmer, or steam table, and served with the pudding hot, and the ice cream just starting to melt.

It may be an acquired taste, but once your guests get used to it, it'll be very popular. This makes one hotel pan, or about 24 portions. A half of this batch would work in a 9" x 13" heavy porcelain or stainless steel oven pan. It's a little hot and heavy for a thin aluminum pan.

Indian Pudding is also a fine example of the Maillard Reaction. It does not provide char grill marks like a prime steak, or browned crust like whole wheat bread, but the flavor, aroma and light color are all from Professeur Maillard's discovery, and a long time in a slow oven.

1 Gallon	Whole Milk
2 ½ cups	Molasses
½ cup	Sugar
½ stick	Butter
1 Tbs	Ground Ginger
1 Tbs	Ground Cinnamon
1 tsp	Ground Nutmeg
2 ½ cups	Yellow Cornmeal

In a steam jacketed kettle, or double boiler, bring half the milk, all the molasses, sugar, butter and spices to a good simmer. Do not burn. In a separate bowl, mix the rest of the milk, and the cornmeal. Mix really well, and add to the first mixture. Bring to one little boil, try not to burn. Cook this for a while, 10 or 20 minutes, and stir occasionally. Transfer this mixture to a sprayed hotel pan. Make sure the pan is deep enough so that it won't spill over the edge when you stir. Cover the Indian Pudding with parchment paper, and the whole pan with aluminum foil.

Bake at about 350 degrees for 1 ½ to 2 hours. Serve right away, or more likely, allow to cool. This will take a while. Reheat in a double boiler, or in the oven, and keep hot for service.

Indian Pudding is best served hot, with a scoop of vanilla ice cream, or some whipped cream.

Irish Soda Bread

Yields 2 x 9" loaves, or 20 rolls

Our traditional American meal for St. Patrick's Day is Corned Beef and Cabbage, with Irish Soda Bread. Well, maybe a Rueben on rye bread, but here's soda bread in any case. Soda bread is a great, healthful addition to a menu at any time of the year. The ingredients are simple, low fat, and good for you. This recipe makes for loaves, or rolls, with a fine thick crust, and deliciously textured center. It stores very well in a plastic bag, and the flavor improves with a day or two. There are few breads which will match Irish Soda Bread for toasting.

This recipe is very easy to make, and good breads can be made with about 10 minutes work, including clean up. The combination of the acid from buttermilk, with the alkaline from baking soda creates the light airy bread, so no time is required for resting or developing the dough. Lowering the oven temperature during baking will make for a crust which is thick, and tender to the bite.

It is easy to personalize these breads or rolls, with dried fruit or seeds in the bread, and with simple garnishes on top, before baking. The flour may be altered to your tastes, by replacing some of the flour with oats, or wheat germ. These are great rolls for brunch, toasted, and served with smoky bacon and scrambled eggs. Change it around for bread that is unique to your family.

4 cups	Whole wheat flour
4 cups	All-purpose flour
2 tsp	Salt
2 tsp	Baking soda
½ stick	Butter
Buttermilk	1 quart

In a large bowl, combine the dry ingredients and sift to keep out horrible lumps of baking soda. Add the butter, crumbling with your fingers as you would for pie dough, leaving pea sized chunks. Add the buttermilk, and mix until all the flour is incorporated. Remove to a lightly floured board. Knead by hand until the dough is well blended. Cut the dough in half, and form a ball with one of the pieces. Add raisins, caraway seeds, dried cranberries, or currants to part of the dough, if you wish. Place on a baking sheet. Cut the remaining dough into 8 or 10 pieces, and form into little rolls. Place on a second baking pan.

Lightly brush the bread, and rolls, with water, and garnish the tops by dusting with flour, wheat germ, oats, or dried herbs. Cut a cross into each piece of dough.

Place in an oven preheated to 400 degrees. After 10 minutes, turn down the heat to 325. The rolls will be done in about 30 minutes, and the bread will be done in about 50 minutes. Allow to cool on the pan. Either serve immediately, or place in a bag, at room temperature, to store for a day or two. Best served warmed up, or toasted

Penne with Roasted Tomatoes, Portabellas, and Pesto

Roasting fresh Roma plum tomatoes creates one of the best flavors and aromas around. Your kitchen will smell like summer. It is even better if you grow them yourself. This creates a great Umami flavor that is indescribable and delicious.

Makes 12 entrée servings

1 each	Fresh Garlic Knob
8 ounces	Fresh Basil Leaves
2 ounces	XVOO
2 ounces	Pinole Nuts (pine nuts)
3 pounds	Penne Pasta
2 ounces	XVOO
3 pounds	Fresh Roma Tomatoes
4 ounces	Garlic fresh peeled
1 pound	Portabella Mushrooms, halved and sliced
3 Tbs	Shredded Parmesan Cheese
2 tsp	Chopped Flat Parsley

Cut the garlic knob in half, through the cloves, and place on a small pan in a hot oven, with a little bit of oil. Roast for 30 minutes until it is browned a little, and soft.

Trim the basil from the stems, wash and dry on paper towels.

Put the basil in a blender, squeeze the garlic meat out of the skins into the basil, and add the pine nuts. Pulse a little, the puree by adding the Extra Virgin Olive Oil in a drizzle. Stop halfway through and scrape the blender bowl so it'll all be pureed. When it is pureed, use a plastic scraper to put in a bowl to cover and refrigerate. (this may also be made with garlic scapes, shallot scapes, or ramps, instead of, or in addition to the basil)

Cook pasta for half the time indicated on package. Drain pasta and drizzle with about 1 tbsp. olive oil to prevent sticking. Do not rinse. Place pasta on sheet pans or hotel pans and cool. Do not rinse the pasta, and do not overcook, as it will continue to cook for a short time on the sheet pan. Once cool, use within one hour or store in bags or sealed plastic container and refrigerate.

Cut tomatoes in halves. Toss with garlic and remaining oil and roast in 450°F oven for about a half hour, until they begin to brown. Turn occasionally they are roasting. Cool, and cut into quarters. Refrigerate until needed.

At service, reheat the penne in boiling water. Drain in a large colander. In a large sauté pan, brown the sliced Portabella mushrooms in a little olive oil. When the mushrooms start to brown, add a kitchen spoonful of roasted tomatoes, a half spoon of pesto, some Parmesan and a little parsley. When this is very, toss with enough of the reheated pasta for your guests and serve.

Argentinian Chimichurri Sauce:

Makes about a quart of sauce

This is a great side topping for grilled steak, chicken, or fish. It is good in small quantities on a spoon. The simplicity of this sauce means that all of the flavors come together over time, and it develops into an intense Umami addition to whatever dish you are making that evening.

It is most important to use fresh and high quality ingredients when making a simple sauce like this. Only use fresh garlic knobs, not canned minced garlic. Shallots are much better than large sweet onions, as their flavor is much more concentrated.

And especially, only use the finest vinegar you can find. Even though it is only a small amount in the sauce, the vinegar may define the flavors. A great red wine vinegar, or sherry vinegar will create a great sauce. A cheap distilled "red wine" vinegar will only detract from all the other flavors.

8 ounces	Fresh flat parsley, washed, stemmed and chopped
1 ounce	Fresh oregano leaves, chopped
2 knobs	Fresh garlic
4 ounces	Shallots, peeled and minced
2 ounces	Anchovy paste
	Freshly ground black pepper
1 Tbs	Dry red chili flakes
4 ounces	Good red wine or sherry vinegar
4 ounces	Fresh squeezed lemon juice
12 ounces	Extra virgin olive oil

Wash the fresh herbs, and remove the stems. Dry a little between paper towels so they are not at all wet, and chop.

Separate the cloves from the knobs of garlic, and peel. Mince very fine. Do the same for the shallots. As fine a mince as you can get. Pot the anchovy paste in a large bowl, and add the shallots and onions. Mix a little, and then add the chili flakes.

Add the good vinegar, and lemon juice, and stir well, so the anchovy paste is well incorporated. Add the chopped herbs and mix well.

When this looks good, drizzle in the Extra Virgin Olive Oil while stirring to make the sauce. Use only the highest quality oil, a peppery flavor is better for this sauce.

This sauce will keep in the cooler for up to 7 days. Use as a side dressing for grilled meats or vegetables.

CHAPTER 4

What Goes Into Great Food

What is umami?

Umami is a taste. It is called the "fifth taste," after salty, sweet, bitter, and sour. There are actually many different taste receptors on the tongue. Umami is the product of glutamates, which are naturally occurring amino acids. The knowledge of which foods contain the most umami flavor will help any cook make great-tasting food.

What is the Maillard reaction?

This is a chemical process occurring between amino acids, reducing sugars, and sometimes heat. It causes browning, plus delicious aroma and taste. Understanding Maillard is a key to making great-tasting food. The difference between Maillard and caramelization is something that every cook worth his or her salt should understand.

Why are ratios important?

Add too much celery to a dish, and it becomes a celery dish. Too much cumin, and it just tastes bad. Add the right amount of either, however, and the dish is delicious. This applies to everything you make. Just as baking is considered both a science and an art, all cooking should be considered a blend of ratios, ingredients, and techniques. Get them all right at the right time, and your dish is great.

Why are reductions important?

Good flavors in combination with other good flavors become great flavors. Great flavors intensified by reduction can help make great dishes. Without the proper ratios, however, reductions can be a detriment. Too much of the best wine reduction will make a sauce that only tastes of sharp red wine. The proper amount of red wine reduction will make the rest of the sauce or dish perfect. Use reductions wisely.

Why is muscle memory important?

One of the rules of great food is "Make what you know." You have a chance of making a great dish the first time, but until you have made all the mistakes and made the recipe enough times to master it, you will not have a great dish you can make all the time. This is "muscle memory," and it is the same for a cook as for a shortstop who constantly practices the double play, the soprano who constantly practices high C, and the boxer who is always working on his right-left combination. Do it again and again, and your muscles will remember how. Learn to make that recipe perfectly, and then do it again and again a hundred times. You might have one great dish.

Muscle memory is not just the physical aspect of, say, slicing an onion. It is also the memory developed over years of making a dish. The combinations of flavors, the ratios of ingredients, the nuances of great food are all developed over many years. Only when we've made a dish innumerable times can we say we have it down.

For instance, in doing sauté work in a very hot pan, there is a fine line between brown and burnt. You don't just see that line, you smell it. You hear it. After you've cooked that same dish a lot, it becomes second nature to turn down the heat just at the right time—just before the object in the pan is done. Muscle memory involves your eyes, your ears, and your nose. All your senses are acting in sync.

Why do we have to learn how to write recipes?

If you don't write them down, they'll die with you. By writing recipes, you are helping to keep a culinary tradition alive—*your* culinary tradition.

Most folks have a hard time learning how to write recipes. They get caught up in the minutia and can't get past the amounts or the exact temperatures. This is cooking, not baking. It is a little science and a lot of art. You don't have to be exact.

Little Things that contribute to Great Food

The good cooks among us know of techniques and flavor combinations that produce far superior dishes. These are not just recipes but certain combinations and methods that increase the many facets of a recipe, creating great food.

There are two very important terms to learn: *Umami* and *the Maillard reaction*, both of which have a great influence on the reasons people like our food. When you learn more about both of these terms, you will realize that they are part of the cooking repertoire of every good chef—and that you already use these techniques regularly.

As a cook, one learns techniques that will enhance the flavors of a dish. If this were not the case, everyone'd just be boiling stuff, and we'd be out of jobs. In the course of things, however, we learn to sear, sauté, broil, and otherwise bring color to our products, imparting rich flavors that set us apart. We learn to combine flavors and use our own special additions so our guests will enjoy their meals.

Most cooks believe that the act of imparting color is caramelization. Caramelization is, in fact, the browning of sugars. Almost all menus talk of caramelization. Folks'll say they caramelize their onions for soups or steaks. They make caramelized carrots, parsnips, butternut squash. They speak of bread crust as nicely caramelized. If they are talking about the color caramel, they are correct. But in a more educated setting, they would realize they are not talking about caramelization but about the Maillard reaction. "Nine-hour caramelized onions" are browned according to Professor Maillard's discovery.

Louis Camille Maillard was a French chemist and physician who lived in the early part of the 20th century. His work was mainly concentrated on kidney diseases, he was instrumental in studying and documenting the reaction between amino acids and sugars. This "non-enzymatic browning" discovery was named after Proffesseur Maillard. We cooks thank him for clarifying what cooks have known for centuries.

People think that the complex flavors we create are just combinations of ingredients. It is not as simple as that. It has been shown scientifically that there are certain absolute reasons why foods react to our culinary techniques and tastes better for it. There has been a collaboration between chefs and scientists for many years to understand exactly what is going on.

In order to illustrate the reaction, I will write a little later about maple syrup. The color in maple syrup is one of the best illustrations of the Maillard reaction. Maple syrup is a favorite ingredient, as you'll see from the recipes.

In the early 1900s, Japanese scientists worked with cooks on a project to define what was long thought of as a "fifth taste.". This taste was described as *umami* (pronounced *OO-Mommy*), and it was defined as "deliciousness." Other English translations could be "brothy," "meaty," or "savory." The difference between good food and great food may be simply a few minor ingredients added to enhance all the flavors. It's not just a matter of adding salt.

Ratios cannot be underrated in the making of great food. Most cooks understand that baking is part science and part art, but they think that cooking is all art. If we approach our recipes with a little bit of scientific understanding, we'll find that the ratios between all the ingredients create new tastes that are developed by combinations of flavors. Ratios are little bit of science in the sauté pan.

Reductions may take place all throughout the cooking process. This is not just a "Cabernet reduction," as one will see on many simple menus. This is perhaps sweating those mushrooms to create a deep-down delicious newly formed ingredient. This is perhaps cooking veal stock into demi-glace, thus enhancing all the flavors in that stock: tomato, onion, celery, veal bones, and brown roux. The resulting sauce should not taste like any of those individual ingredients; it should be a newly developed, deep rich taste that will enhance whatever sauce or dish it becomes part of.

Muscle memory is not just about being able to chop an onion perfectly all the time. It includes recognizing the flavor or a sauce when the sauce is half done. It takes many hundreds or thousands of times making that same sauce successfully to be able to know what it should taste like at all parts of the cooking process.

Part of muscle memory is the educated palate. It is a misconception that an educated palate involves finely developed taste buds so that one may taste wine and recognize the exact vineyard and hill the grapes came from. A person with an educated palate has tasted many kinds of food—bad, good, and great—and can recognize nuances because he or she knows that the nuances are important. Her or his taste buds may be just as good as anyone else's, but they've been there, done that, and know the difference. After you've tasted great onion soup fifty times, you know what to look for. That's muscle memory.

Corn and Avocado Relish

Makes about 12 servings

Fresh summer corn is something we look forward to each year. This recipe is a way to expand your corn repertoire, making the most delicious salad or relish, and keeping it around in the refrigerator to add to all sorts of plates. The freshness of the ingredients is the measure of quality in the final dish.

It is also a dish you may personalize in any manner. By simply cutting the vegetables a little different you may make this your own dish. You may also change the ingredients to make it a signature family recipe.

1 each	Yellow, green, and red bell peppers
4 each	Jalapeno peppers
1 bunch	Scallions
2 medium	Red Onions
2 each	Cucumbers
4 each	Ripe plum tomatoes
1 knob	Fresh garlic
½ cup	Fresh cilantro, chopped
12 each	Fresh mint leaves
2 cans	Black eyed peas, drained
2 cans	Black beans, drained
12 ears	Fresh sweet corn
8 oz	Zesty Italian dressing

(3 oz very good red wine vinegar steeped with ½ tsp garlic powder, dried oregano, dried basil, and 1 tsp chili powder. After 10 minutes add 5 oz XVOO)

Trim and seed the 3 sweet peppers, and chop to a medium dice. Chop the jalapenos, being careful not to touch your eyes, leaving in the seeds if you want this stuff hot. Slice the scallions thin. Peel the red onions, and chop as fine as you can. Peel the cucumbers, and remove the seeds. Cut into whatever shape you'd like. Wash and trim the plum tomatoes, and coarsely dice.

Cut the garlic knobs in half, and roast in a 400° oven with a little olive oil for about 20 minutes, until they are soft and a little browned. Squeeze out the cloves, and chop. Chop the cilantro, and add all this to the tomato mixture. Drain and rinse the peas and beans. If using dried beans that you are going to cook, make sure they are well cooled before adding to the relish.

Put on a big pot of water to boil. Go outside and pick 12 fat ears of corn. Shuck them, and put them in boiling water for 10 minutes. Run under cool water, maybe using some ice, to quickly cool them. Cut the kernels off the ears with a sharp knife and add to the relish. Garnish with a little mint.

Let above marinate for at least 2 hours overnight is better. Finish with a chopped or sliced ripe avocado.

Grilled Maple and Balsamic Glazed Pork Chops

Makes 6 servings

There are certain flavors, in combination, which create new and interesting tastes. Orange juice, Maple Syrup, and Balsamic vinegar, reduced in the right ratios, will create a new taste quite different than any of the ingredients. This recipe is equally as good with chicken, duck breast, or London broil.

The Fall Vegetable Hash is a great dish to have around the kitchen. It may be made up one day, and kept for reheat for several days, if the vegetables are not overcooked. The second reheating should be with very high heat, so the surface browns nicely.

2 each	Sweet Potatoes
1 each	Butternut Squarsh
2 each	Yukon Gold Potato
4 cloves	Whole Peeled Garlic
2 each	Carrots
1 each	Turnips
2 each	Parsnips
1 each	Onion, chopped
2 ounces	Olive Oil
8 ounces	Pure Maple Syrup
4 ounces	Balsamic Vinegar
4 ounces	Orange Juice
1 ounces	Minced Garlic
12 each	Bone in Pork Chops

Clean and peel the vegetables, in any ratio you'd like. They are all good by themselves or in combination. Sweet Potatoes by themselves are a major source of Umami flavor. Sauté the onions in olive oil until they start to brown, cover with the other vegetables and place in a very hot oven. Stir occasionally. Take out of the oven when they are browned, and starting to get soft. Don't overcook them or the sweet potatoes and squash will turn to mush.

In a small saucepan, combine the Pure Maple Syrup, vinegar, and orange juice. Bring to a boil and simmer over low heat until mixture is reduced by half, about 15 minutes. Remove from heat and let cool.

Grill the pork chops over an open flame for 5 minutes on each side, or on a very hot heavy pan, for color. Brush some of the maple-balsamic glaze on the pork chops and finish in an oven at 350º until they are just done. Keep warm.

At service, put the pork chops in the oven to get real hot. Put enough of the vegetable mixture in the oven. Serve when well browned, and very hot. Add chopped scallions for color, and some hot pepper for flavor, if you wish, at the end of the cooking process. Serve the pork chops with a little of the maple glaze, surrounded by the vegetables.

Cider Braised Pot Roast

Makes about 18 servings

Good pot roast is simple to make, but hard to make great. You'll need two large pots, one with a very heavy bottom. The meat, when done, can be held for several days, and will improve if it is held in the cooking liquid. Trimming is easier if done when the meat has completely cooled. If the roast is properly cooked, it will slice into perfect portions, with very little shredding, or other waste. It makes great sandwiches.

10 pounds	Beef Top Butt Sirloin, or Chuck Roast
1 quart	Low sodium beef broth
1 quart	Water
4 stalks	Trimmed Celery
2 large	Onions
2 each	Peeled Carrots
1 quart	Fresh Apple Cider
1 TBS	Fresh Sage
1 pound	Peeled Shallots
4 each	Peeled Carrots
4 each	Peeled Parsnips
4 stalks	Trimmed Celery
4 each	Yukon Gold Potatoes, unpeeled, halved

Cut your meat in two pieces, or more, depending on how large a piece of beef you get. It is hard to handle more than 5 pounds at a time when it is hot. Don't trim the fat. In a large pot, boil several gallons of water, and place the meat in the boiling water. Remove after only a few minutes. This effectively seals every single corner of the meat.

Dry the meat, and then brown the meat on all sides in a large, heavy, deep pan. Remove from the pan, and sweat the onion, peeled carrots and the celery in the same pan until they start to brown. Add the water, beef base, sage, and apple cider, and bring to a boil. Return the beef to the liquid, and simmer for 2-3 hours, or until the internal temperature is at least 180 degrees. If in doubt, give it another half hour. Remove from the pan, and allow to cool in a deep pan.

Strain the cooking liquid into a large sauce pan. Bring to a boil, skim the surface, and thicken slightly with a cornstarch or arrowroot slurry, or a little roux. The consistency should be rather thin and smooth.

Wash and peel all the root vegetables. Cut them into different shapes for a nice look. Put the diced, or sliced, onions in a large roasting pan, or sheet pan with a little olive oil. When browned a little, add the other vegetables and roast until they all start to brown. Toss them once in a while. Pour the thinnish sauce on these vegetables and cook until they are just done.

At this point, pour on this vegetable and sauce mixture on the cooked beef, so that the beef is covered. Cool, cover, and refrigerate at least overnight.

CHAPTER 5

The Rubber Chicken Dinner

Ask politicians or public figures about the many dinners they must attend each year. These are very important events for anyone like a college president, city council member, or CEO. To be seen and heard in public gives you the chance to garner support for whatever endeavor you are working on. The dinners are free (to them), and the booze is flowing.

There is a downside to this gala-filled and extravagant life. These dinners have a name. The name is not complimentary. It is quite descriptive and generally accurate. This is the "rubber chicken circuit."

You go to these fine catering halls or public venues and dine with a few hundred of your peers. The conversation, camaraderie, and fellowship are great, but the food sucks. Oh, the plates sure are pretty, with fine garnishes and fancy sauce painting, but nothing more is expected except that the food will suck. Maybe the salad will be okay, maybe the water will be cold, but the chicken will be rubbery and oversalted, however perfect it may look on the plate.

That is because the folks who put on these dinners are more concerned with plating the food than with making great food. All they have to do is salt the crap out of everything, and the customers will think it is just fine. All they have to do is make the plates be gorgeous—with perfect little micro garnishes, glazes brushed on the plates, foams and crisps—and the person paying the bill will think it is just fine. Mr. Johnson will turn to Ms. Smith on his left and say, "My, this plate is just beautiful." Ms. Smith will agree and add, "Yes, and the chicken is almost not rubber this time!"

Perhaps if the platers would learn to become great cooks and work on their culinary skills instead of their visual skills, they wouldn't need superfluous little foams and micro garnishes that add nothing to the dish. Perhaps their food would be pretty and delicious on its own. Perhaps Ms. Smith would turn to Mr. Johnson and say, "This is the most delicious chicken I've had this season!"

If cooks at home and at work learn to make better food, there will be less salt, less fat, and fewer superfluous garnishes on plates. We will be eating tastier, healthier meals, and politicians will actually look forward to the political dinner circuit. Garnishes and good plating are very nice, but they pale in comparison to great food.

CHAPTER 6

The Maillard Reaction

Now let's talk about the Maillard reaction (also called the Maillard effect). This is a chemical reaction between amino acids and a reducing sugar, usually requiring heat. It's a phenomenon that's been known in a practical sense since ancient times. In the food-service industry, the Maillard reaction is responsible for many of our favorite flavors and aromas, including toasted bread, malted barley (beer), roasted or seared meat, roasted coffee, and chocolate. It is responsible for the color and flavor of browned onions that make French onion soup so good.

This is a chemical reaction between amino acids and a reducing sugar, usually requiring heat. In cooking, Maillard is responsible for color, flavor, and aroma in great, highly desired dishes. It causes browning, plus delicious aroma and taste. Understanding Maillard is a key to making great-tasting food. The difference between Maillard and caramelization is something that every cook worth his or her salary should learn.

Caramelization is quite different. It produces a brown color and new flavors due to the burning of sugar, but it is one-dimensional and is not responsible for the complex flavors that we know from our learned culinary techniques. Caramelization tastes like browned sugar: one dimension.

The Maillard reaction is different in that it involves amino acids reacting with the reducing sugars present in many food products. It is a form of nonenzymatic browning. For instance, caramel made from milk and sugar in candy is flavored in a large amount through this reaction. One of our favorite products, maple syrup, gains its colors entirely from the Maillard reaction. The light amber color of maple syrup from early-season boilings compares to the deep dark brown of late season syrup because of the differences in the sap working in a chemical process while boiled.

Although good cooks have been taking advantage of this reaction forever for flavor and appearance, it is named after the French chemist Louis-Camille Maillard, who discovered the reaction while researching sugars and amino acids as part of a study of kidney disorders for his PhD thesis.

Bakers, of all the culinary artists, know Maillard best. Bread has proteins (gluten) and sugars (starch). A baker's mastery of the reaction will result in the color and aroma of fresh bread. The reaction also happens at lower temperatures. Dry-cured Serrano ham, for instance, never sees heat. It's only salted for two weeks, rinsed, and then hung to dry for about a year. Yet a Maillard reaction occurs, slowly, until the ham takes on a brown color and develops a delicious aroma.

We love the Maillard reaction—its flavors, colors, and especially aromas. Go to work in a bakery. The first couple of days, the aroma of fresh-baked bread, muffins, and Danish is overwhelming in its deliciousness. Ten years later, the aroma is just as good. You never tire of the aroma of fresh-baked goods.

Raw meat has little flavor and almost no aroma—but when seared, the outside of the meat becomes brown and flavorful. This is not a matter of sugars browning but the Maillard reaction between the reducing sugars (glucose) in the meat and the amino acids naturally occurring, especially in red meat. The bad taste and smell of burnt eggs and burnt broccoli are unfortunate examples of the Maillard reaction.

If not for Professor Maillard, we would think that those great Kansas City barbecue guys are just a bunch of yahoo cooks. Now we recognize that the intricate and well-developed techniques used in the slow braising of barbecued meats owes its appeal to the Maillard effect.

It is necessary that good cooks develop their knowledge of recipes and ingredients. They also need to understand why these combinations, plus the methods used to create the dish, make for a great recipe. Knowing about umami flavors is as useful as understanding salty, sweet, and tart, and bitter. It is good to know that a certain way to sear meat, or to bake or toast bread, is a chemical process and not just an application of heat.

The knowledge of, and use of, umami and the Maillard reaction will create different and much more flavorful tastes and aromas. Recipes featuring umami and the Maillard reaction are easy to find on the Internet. These are not exotic and difficult-to-market recipes, but everyday items that sell well.

Understanding Maillard's role in our cooking techniques enables us to deeply add to our flavors, colors, and aromas. It creates universally delicious food and goes a long way toward making good food great.

Caramelization vs. the Maillard Reaction

Caramelizing is the browning or burning of sugars. It is temperature dependent and occurs at over 300 degrees for sucrose. Both caramelization and the Maillard reaction can be described as nonenzymatic browning; the difference is that caramelization involves the breaking down of sugar by heat instead of reaction with amino acids, as in the Maillard reaction.

What is described on a menu as "caramelized onions" is probably not. There may be some caramelization, but the slow cooking of onions for great onion soup depends mainly on the Maillard reaction for the color and taste that make great flavors and aromas.

Maple Syrup and the Maillard Reaction

Note the color development of maple syrup. Maple sap comes out of the tree as a barely sweet water. It has no color; it's just real good-tasting water. It takes forty or fifty gallons of maple water to make one gallon of syrup, at which point it is deliciously golden.

As the sap cooks, it begins to brown. This is from the Maillard reaction. Heat reacts with amino acids to begin producing flavor, color, and aroma. By the time the sap is half cooked—that is, say, 20:1—it is browning nicely and has a delicious flavor, even though it is still quite watery and nowhere near a syrup consistency. It is at most 212 degrees, not even close to a caramelizing temperature.

In fact, maple syrup does not ever reach a temperature over 220 degrees. The color begins to develop halfway through the evaporating process, when the temperature is at 212. Even the simplest of caramelized sugars—caramelized fructose—does not begin to take effect until 230 degrees.

Using the Maillard Reaction to Make Food Great

Most dishes will improve with the judicious use of the Maillard reaction in their methods. The color produced, plus the flavor and aroma, can go a long way toward making a dish great. In addition, of course, the dish has to be made from good ingredients, be pleasing to the eye, and be in such proportions as to be great. We will be looking at onion soup later as a definition of a great food.

Think of the difference between ravioli and bread. These are two totally different tastes from the same products: flour and water. The only difference is that ravioli is boiled and kept white, while bread is baked and gets browned through the Maillard reaction. The ravioli needs a filling that is highly flavored and a sauce to make it a very good dish. But bread just needs to be baked.

Bacon Jam

Makes about a quart of bacon jam

This may sound like a very strange thing to make, one that will not be at all tasty or popular, but do not be deceived. Bacon Jam is one of the great products to keep in your fridge. This is a great accompaniment to any roasted meat, on a Charcuterie or Cheese platter, or plain on toast.

2 pounds	Bacon ends and pieces
2 pounds	Onions, diced
4 ounces	Garlic cloves
2 cups	Coffee, brewed
2 ounces	Brown Sugar
6 ounces	Pure Maple Syrup
1 dash or more	Hot Sauce
8 ounces	Good Apple Cider Vinegar

Fry the bacon in a large heavy pan until they are crisp and well rendered. Add the onions, and continue to cook until they start to wilt. Add the garlic and cook on medium heat until it smells real good.

Add the coffee, brown sugar, maple syrup (use more if you like), a little of your favorite hot sauce, and the (good) cider vinegar. Continue to cook on medium heat.

Cook about 2 hours, adding water as necessary to keep the Bacon Jam from drying out. At this point transfer to stainless steel, and cool overnight. The next day, remove the bacon fat from the top of the jam. You may chop in a food processor, or not.   Keep in the cooler for up to 7 days.

This is an example of a fine mixture of Umami ingredients (rule #1 – anything goes better with bacon), the Maillard slow cooking technique, and the reduction of ingredients.

Roast Brisket with Wild Mushroom Sauce

makes 20 servings

This is a great dish when the weather cools off a bit. It is hard to do well, as you need to develop all the flavors by browning in the correct manner, to trim, and cut the finished product. When done well, it is a great seller and is easy to reheat and serve.

1 each	Fresh beef brisket (not corned beef, but fresh brisket)
1 quart	Water
2 Tbs	Oregano dried
1 Tbs	Garlic powder
4 Tbs	Shallots minced
4 oz	Garlic fresh minced
3 pounds	Shiitake mushrooms
3 pounds	Portabella mushrooms
3 pounds	Crimini mushrooms
8 oz	Very Good Dry Red wine
½ gallon	Beef stock

Remove the brisket from its bag, and trim some of the fat off the top. Rub the raw brisket with oregano and garlic powder liberally. Let sit, covered, in a refrigerator at least one night. You may add any other dry spices of your choice.

Roast the brisket at 325 in a conventional oven, in a pan with some water, covered with foil, for about 2 ½ hours. Uncover, and roast for an additional 30 minutes to brown. Remove from the oven, place in another pan, and allow to cool.

Trim the bottoms off of the mushrooms. Wash them, and dry as best you can on a sheet pan with paper towels. Slice pretty thick, or half, or however you want to cut them. Brown them in a separate heavy bottomed pan and put to the side to cool.

Remove and save the water from the first roasting pan. Brown the shallots and garlic in this pan, scraping up all the little bits that are stuck to the pan. Deglaze the pan with some good red wine and the original water, scraping the bottom well. Reduce for a while, and add the beef stock. Bring to a boil, and strain into a saucepan.

Thicken the beef stock with some cornstarch or arrowroot slurry to keep this gluten free. Simmer for at least ½ hour. Keep rather thin. Strain this over the mushrooms for a good sauce. Pour this over the brisket and keep in the cooler at least overnight. Use the beef within one week. Trim the brisket, and slice and serve with mushroom sauce.

CHAPTER 7

Introducing Umami

In the early twentieth century, Japanese scientists began investigating why they thought certain foods made other foods taste better. Umami as a separate taste was first identified in 1908 by Kikunae Ikeda at Tokyo Imperial University, while he was researching the strong flavor of seaweed broth. You've got to hand it to those great Japanese scientists. They came up with this inventive idea using seaweed, of all things.

These scientists strove to define what was long thought of as a "fifth taste." Ikeda isolated glutamates as the chemical responsible for this flavor. This led to the commercial production of monosodium glutamate (MSG), a processed chemical compound that can have a detrimental effect on one's health. Poor cooks learned that they could use this stuff indiscriminately, and they overloaded food with MSG, under the erroneous impression that it made stuff taste better.

The middle part of the word is *sodium*. You eat too much sodium, you get a headache. So pouring on the MSG will give you the classic "MSG headache." This is not a good way to find umami. Overuse of MSG led to a great backlash and the words "No MSG" on most menus in Chinese restaurants.

Good cooks the world over have known that certain foods enhance the flavor of other foods in combination and have decried the use of chemical additions. They know they possess much higher powers than can be found in a chemical powder.

Since 1908, the types of foods that have high quantities of glutamates have been codified, and a good list of umami ingredients has been created. Here is a short list of some high-glutamate ingredients:

miso	soy sauce
beef broth	tomato ketchup
Parmesan cheese	sauerkraut
anchovy paste	vegemite
(see Worcestershire sauce)	(Australian yeast extract)
tuna	blue cheese
seaweed	shiitake mushrooms
crimini mushrooms	sweet potatoes
oysters	tomato juice

When these foods are used in certain ways, the glutamates are released, imparting the fifth flavor of umami to a dish.

There are certain ingredients good cooks have been using without recognizing that the umami connection is the reason food tastes better. Worcestershire sauce, ketchup, soy sauce, and Parmesan cheese are used extensively as flavor enhancers. The umami taste is created in each of these products by glutamates being freed and enhanced in the cooking and fermentation involved in the production of these items.

More information about umami is easily found on the Internet. Umami is a taste and an important culinary property, one that no good cook can ignore. This is a serious subject. Of course, there are a few umami jokes that need be told:

Umami so fat when she sits around the house, she sits around the house.
Umami so skinny she only got one stripe on her pajamas.
Umami so dumb it takes her an hour and a half to watch *60 Minutes.*
Umami so old when she was in school there was no history class.

With a little research, though, you may find out which of the ingredients you use on a regular basis will produce umami. Using these ingredients in the proper combinations may simply make your customers appreciate your menu.

The previous list of umami ingredients is a simple way to add flavor to all your dishes. A little investigation will add innumerable umami ingredients, and you'll find you've been adding them to your dishes for years. Look it up. Adding umami ingredients, in combination and in concentration, is one of the primary ways to make good food great.

That simple sauce for, say, pot roast is kind of flavorless. Most folks'll add a whole lot of salt and think that makes it taste great. They're wrong; it'll just make it taste salty. But add a spoonful of tomato paste, a sprinkle of Parmesan cheese, and a sautéed chopped mushroom, boil, and strain, and you'll have a great sauce with no additional salt. Understanding umami is a necessary skill for making great food, especially for those who should be on low-sodium diets.

CHAPTER 8

Two Cooks

Think of two cooks making beef barley soup. Both use the same recipe. First guy cuts some nice fresh mirepoix, dices beef, slices mushrooms, and gets some stock and barley together. He puts all this in a steam-jacketed kettle, mushes it up and gets it real hot, adds a bunch of salt, and voilà! He's got soup. It's nutritious, wholesome, and needs salt. Maybe some saltine crackers. A little pepper wouldn't hurt.

The lady in the other kitchen uses the same ingredients. But she browns her mirepoix in a heavy pan and then deglazes the pan. She browns the beef chunks, trying to get as much color as she can. She deglazes the pan by cooking the mushrooms in the beef drippings. She adds some broth made from bones she roasted. Then, she adds a few minor ingredients—a little tomato puree, some Worcestershire sauce, and a kitchen spoon of Parmesan. One boil, skim, she's done.

Same recipe, different methods, and some very small additions of minor ingredients has turned the good soup into a great soup. Salt? Salt? We don't need no stinkin' salt!

The second cook used the Maillard reaction and added some umami ingredients. Her soup now has great color, flavor, and aroma. No extra money, just good cooking techniques make this a great dish. It tastes great without the extra salt.

What Is Great Food?

Great food is rare. Great food is made by cooks who know these little tricks that bring out flavor, aroma, and color in any dish. Most cooks who make great food do not specifically know how their food becomes great; they just know that if they perform certain little actions or use a little of certain ingredients, the dish is vastly improved.

Understanding umami and the Maillard reaction are key to making great food. The minute differences in ingredients and methods made by a cook who understands these two principles will turn good food great. Great food needs little salt. The flavors and aroma come not just from the primary ingredients but also those small additions of flavor and those methods that bring out taste, texture, color, and aroma.

Presentation

This is very important. How food looks on a plate will enhance or detract from your guest's perception of the dish. But presentation can only go so far. Good food presented in an artistic and incredible manner will still be good food. Good food presented with all the modern garnishes will still need salt. Great food presented in a plain manner will still be great food.

Making Great Food

Understanding the Maillard reaction and knowing which ingredients add umami to your food are essential to making great food. Perhaps the differences between good food and great food are small, but the end result is great.

There are some additional areas of discussion in this book, such as ratios, recipes, presentation, and menu descriptions. Each of these is important in how your guests judge your dishes. Umami and the Maillard reaction are more difficult to explain, so I started there. If you know what umami ingredients are and how to control and enhance food using the Maillard reaction, your menu will improve dramatically.

It is even better if you can teach your staff to use these ingredients and techniques to improve all food that comes out of your kitchen. As appearance is a major part of any menu, I will touch on kitchen cleanliness, at least in the basic areas that will make a dramatic difference in how your guests judge your dishes.

We all make a few great dishes. Maybe this little book will help you understand why your great dishes are great and the others are just really good. With a little understanding about umami, Maillard, and a few other important points, your good food can taste great.

Mushroom Beef and Barley Soup

makes about 12 servings

Soup may be the most difficult type of food to make great. Good soup is easy, great soup takes some skill.

This soup can be great, and is also gluten free, as there is no flour involved in searing the beef. Other cuts of beef may be used, such as hanger steak, or ribeye cap, but avoid the lean meats such as bottom round. Be careful to cook the barley separately, as it is easier to calculate the correct amount for the soup after it has been cooked.

1 pound	Beef boneless Short Ribs
2 ounces	Olive Oil
3 ounces	Shallots, minced
4 ounces	White Mushrooms, sliced
4 ounces	Shiitake mushrooms, sliced
1 Tbs	Fresh thyme, chopped
2 each	Plum tomatoes, chopped
1 quart	Water
8 ounces	Dry red wine
2 pints	Beef broth
2 pints	Water
1 each	Bay leaves
1 ounce	Balsamic vinegar
4 ounces	Barley
1 Tbs	Flat Parsley, chopped
1 Tbs	Ketchup
1 Tbs	Worcestershire Sauce
1 Tbs	Parmesan Cheese
4 ounces	Sour cream for garnish

Sear the ribs on all sides until well browned. Remove from pan and set aside. In the same pot, sauté the shallots and half of the mushrooms until browned. Add the thyme and any spices you may like. Pour in the wine and simmer until liquid is reduced by half. Add the broth, water, bay leaf, tomatoes and the ribs; bring to a boil, reduce heat and simmer, covered, for about an hour or more, or until the meat starts to fall from the bone. Remove the ribs from the broth. Let cool, and cut as you wish in strips or cubes.

In a separate pan, sauté the reserved mushrooms until tender. Add the vinegar to the mushrooms, and cook until evaporated. Strain the original sauce over the mushrooms, add the cut up cooked beef, and bring to a boil. Skim the surface and taste the soup. You might at this point want to add some ketchup and other Umami ingredients to enhance the flavor. Boil once again and skim the surface.

In a heavy pan, toast the barley in a little oil until it starts to brown and gets a nutty aroma. Cover with water and cook for about a half hour until it is done. Cool and set aside.

Add some barley to the soup. Let it cook for 10 minutes so you may decide if you want to add more. It'll swell, and you don't want barley stew. The Barley should be more like a garnish than the main ingredient. The main ingredient is the broth.

Serve the soup very hot, and add a little sour cream and parsley to garnish if you'd like.

Lemon Maple Salmon

Makes 6 servings

This is a great, unexpected use for maple syrup. The flavor is intensified by reduction, and the combination of maple, lemon, soy sauce and scallions is delicious. The mild sweetness of the Maple syrup goes well with the tartness of the lemon and the saltiness of the soy sauce.

It is an easy dish to set up and serve on a busy hot line, and will command a very good price for a nice looking plate. This dish can also be made in volume in hotel pans, and will sit very well for a limited time on a buffet line, chafing dish or hot box, say a half hour, making it very useful for high end buffets and weddings menus.

3 each	Lemons
1 cup	Pure Maple Syrup
2 Tbs	Good Cider Vinegar
1 Tbs	Soy Sauce
6 each	Salmon filets, boneless 6 oz
8 oz	Scallions, long sliced

Squeeze the juice from the lemons into a saucepan, and slice the remaining lemons as thin as you can.

Add the maple syrup, the soy sauce, and the vinegar to the lemon juice, bring to a boil and reduce a little.

Set up the salmon in sizzle platters, hotel pans, or sheet pans, depending on the volume. Put a little water under the salmon, and cover with the sliced juiced lemons, and some of the maple sauce.

Bake in a hot oven until the fish is done. You may need to add a little water to the pan, or some marinade while it is cooking, to keep the fish moist. Decoratively top the salmon with long slices of scallion in the last minute of baking, and add any of the maple sauce that you have left, as a final heating before plating the dish.

CHAPTER 9

Basic Great Food Ingredients

Any good food can be made great—not by adding salt or a ton of sugar, but by adhering to some simple rules. A primary rule is knowing where your food comes from.

Most restaurants are more concerned with consistency than with greatness. If they strive for greatness, chances are it'll be great on Tuesday, but only good on Saturday, unless the kitchen staff really know what they're doing. If they strive only for consistency, then they will have consistent good food, never great, and they will pack the joint. This is the culinary business model of most food-service establishments.

We call this style of cooking "truck to plate." You, of course, have heard of the "farm to table" style of menu. Well, most places will buy preprepared food that only needs heating and beautiful plating. They can sell wonderful food that is oversalted, oversugared, and overfatted—and most people will love it. Think of anything that is deep fried, for example.

Back in the day, cooks like this, who relied on premade products, were known as "can openers" or more likely "shoemakers." Nothing bad about a shoemaker, of course, since that is a highly skilled craft, but we don't really think that most shoemakers know much about cooking. (We do hope that lousy workers in the shoemaker field are called "cooks.")

So, knowing your ingredients, knowing their freshness, and knowing where they came from is imperative. We grow plenty of vegetables and herbs, and we eat them fresh to the extreme. If it ain't fresh, it's frozen within twenty minutes of the field. In fact, we label our freezer bags "20-minute corn" or "20-minute green beans," because that's how long it takes to process the product. Put the water on to boil, then go out and pick the ears of corn. We freeze tomatoes raw; they're peeled, trimmed, and juiced slightly and then packed into freezer bags. Opening a bag of fresh frozen tomatoes in January smells like July.

The products you buy from far away are not as fresh, wholesome, or delicious. Lettuce, herbs, and vegetables grown thousands of miles away, in other states or other countries, cannot be nearly as good as something grown locally. Yes, you have to compromise on your ingredients, as you can't buy fresh raspberries in February unless you fly them in from Chile. But you *can* use fresh raspberries frozen in September.

Use the freshest and best ingredients you can. It'll go a long way toward helping your dish go from good to great.

The best way to find great food ingredients is to look at the ingredient label of what you are buying. Simply put, it should be simply put. The fewest ingredients mean the cleanest food. Even better, of course are those items with no ingredients, such as fresh vegetables. But you may want to find frozen vegetables in the middle of the winter, as they will be fresher and more wholesome than produce that has been shipped around the world and has been in cold storage for a very long time.

There are items which you purchase that you'd think, or assume are simple, wholesome foods. Fresh fish. Fresh chickens. Well now, if you look closely at the label of the chicken you're buying, you'll see there is water and "flavorings" added. This means the chicken has been put into a large vacuum tank with a whole lot of other chickens, and a lot of water, salt, sugar, and other "flavorings". This makes the chicken taste better, as it's salty. It makes it a little more tender. It makes it a little more juicy, although the water does cook out of the bird. Mostly, it makes the chicken heavier. So, if you pay $3 a pound for a chicken, you are paying $3 a pound for water, also. Not a great deal. The same process is used on pork and beer.

Fresh and frozen seafood is treated with an ingredient called Trisodium Polyphosphate. This is a salt used to keep the fish fresh looking, and helps to put extra water into the meat. This is used on almost all frozen seafood, and if so, is listed on the label. Fresh seafood will not have this listing, so you'll have to learn which fish are not so treated.

If you want great ingredients, you'll have to do some research. There are many good sources of clean, simple food out there, fresh, frozen and otherwise processed. There are many sources of natural and organic products, more so than ever. All this stuff costs considerably more, but is worth every penny.

CHAPTER 10

Concentrating Flavors

Simply adding good flavors to a dish is not enough. If this is your style, you will be making dishes that are *delicate*. This is another word for *tasteless*.

Taking umami ingredients—such as tomatoes, beef stock, or wine—and cooking them down as a reduction will intensify the flavors. Commercial examples of concentrated umami flavors include ketchup (American umami), Worcestershire sauce (British umami), vegemite (Australian umami), demi-glace, chutney, Stubb's BBQ sauce, and A1 sauce. The more you understand umami, the better and more intense your flavors will be.

Mixing different umami ingredients like mushrooms, broth, and cheeses will intensify the flavors. These ingredients may be a major part of the dish, such as mushrooms in a soup. Or they may be subtle flavors, such as a shot of lemon juice or a little Worcestershire—not enough to change the flavor of the dish, but enough to make all the other ingredients taste better.

Reductions are deceiving. You cook this stuff down, and then you add it to a sauce, which you'd think would unreduce it by dilution. But the new taste is different. Bordelaise sauce is a rather thin sauce that should have a sharp vinegar flavor from reduced wine, but it is a delicious product and extremely difficult to make right. Made correctly, with the proper concentrations of flavor and the proper ratios, it is one of the world's great sauces.

One of the finest products of flavor concentration is béarnaise sauce. Take a simple hollandaise. It is very good with your eggs and ham, on asparagus or broccoli. Now, add a reduction with shallots, wine, and tarragon, and it is better. It is great food. Add the reduction of umami flavors in wine, vinegar, shallots, pepper, and tarragon, and the sauce is unique and outstanding.

CHAPTER 11

Ratios

In creating a dish and writing a recipe, ratios are of extreme importance. The difference between a dish with the addition of some good cheese and a dish that is dominated by cheese is huge.

We have found ourselves in the past adding too much of an ingredient to a dish, just because there is extra stuff on the cutting board. You may have an extra pound of chopped red pepper and nowhere else to use it, and you're afraid of it going to waste. It is your job to find a use for that ingredient, not to add it to the dish you are creating just because it's there. That great dish you are cooking will become a red pepper dish if you add too much.

This is not so foreign to bakers. Bakers are used to using formulas, not recipes. A formula is a specific ratio of ingredients, combined in an exacting sequence, with exact actions, to form a product. Something as simple as a loaf of bread will need to have very specific amounts of flour, water, yeast, and salt, and will need to be worked for a specific amount of time, allowed to rise at a certain temperature, rested and worked in a very precise manner, and baked at a specific temperature.

Follow the formula, and you will have a perfect loaf—the same every time. Any deviations, and it'll be nice bread, but it may not look or taste as good.

The same goes for cooking, but that fact is not often recognized. Most cooks think they can just add stuff, heat it up somehow, and it will all go together to make good food. And that's what they get, if they're lucky—good food. In order to get great food, you need precision in methods, ingredients, and ratios.

That chicken sauté dish made quickly by just anyone on the line is okay. It can be made to look nice and will sell. But that same chicken dish made precisely as defined by a great cook will be great food, and it will command a much greater price.

Maybe that's the definition of great food: good food that commands a great price.

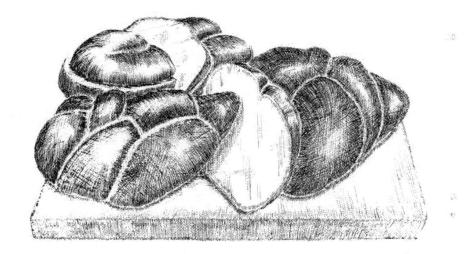

Roast Pork Loin with Maple Water and Mustard

Makes about 24 servings, or one hotel pan

Roast pork loin is an easy thing to cook well. It can be roasted or braised, and is very easy to cut when cooled after roasting. This dish is an easy reheat, and the sauce gets more delicious as it sits with the browned pork loin.

Maple Water is the liquid that comes right out of the tree. For maple syrup it is cooked down from 40 or so gallons, to one gallon. Right from the tree it is also useful, and delicious. It makes great tea, great sauces and this dish is delicious.

1 each	Boneless Pork Loin (about 9 pounds)
4 pounds	Sliced Onions
8 ounces	Whole Grain Mustard
3 quarts	Maple Water

(or out of season, use 2 ½ quarts water and 1 cup Pure Maple Syrup)

Cut the pork loin in half, and in a heavy pan, on high heat, sear the pork loin on every edge very brown. You'll probably have to do each half of your pork loins at a time. Don't worry about the pan being all browned up, this is good flavor for the sauce.

When the pork loins are browned, and put on a separate platter, add all the onions, and sauté over medium to high heat until they are well wilted and getting browned. At this point add the mustard and mush it up a bunch. Add the maple water, or the maple syrup blend, and bring to a boil. Reduce by half. Now you have an oniony broth that is slightly sweet, with a major mustard back up flavor.

Put the pork loins in an oven proof dish with high edges, like a 4" hotel pan, and pour this water on top, to say half cover the pork loins. Roast at 350 degrees, turning once every 15 minutes or so, for about an hour and a half, until the pork loin is about 165 degrees internal temperature.

Remove the pork loin to a storage container, and finish the sauce. Either add a stick of butter, or thicken with a ¼ cup of cornstarch slurry, just enough to give it a sheen, not to thicken. Cook 10 minutes and then pour on the pork loin. Cool, cover, and keep in the refrigerator at least overnight.

To serve the roast, take the pork out of the sauce and slice thin. Put in a pan with lots of onions, and lots of sauce, and reheat. Serve hot or cold as an entrée, or salad, or use in sandwiches.

Chicken Marsala with Grilled Criminis

Makes about 24 servings, or one hotel pan

Criminis, when browned, create a distinct and delicious flavor that cannot be equaled by any other product.

The flavor is intensified while they are browned, and the browning creates a new taste. They have less water content than most other mushrooms, but they are still very difficult to brown. A very hot pan, with the Criminis not touching at all, is the most effective method of browning these mushrooms.

8 pounds	Chicken Breast, boneless, skinless
8 oz	Olive Oil
8 oz	All Purpose Flour
8 oz	Shallots, peeled and sliced
2 pounds	Crimini Mushrooms
8 oz	Scallions
1 pint	Marsala Wine
1 pint	Veloute
5 pounds	Rice
5 pounds	Green Beans

Use about 6 ounces of chicken per guest. No need to pound. Dredge the chicken in flour, and brown in oil as hot as possible (Maillard). Remove chicken from pan, and pour off most of the oil. Sweat the shallots in the same pan. For large quantities, you can just put them in a hot oven, letting them brown well. In fact, you can let them get a little overcooked and dry, it'll help the final result.

Coat the mushrooms very lightly with olive oil, or spray with oil, and grill on chargrill, looking for good marks. If there is no grill is available, then sauté very hot in a pan until they begin to brown. Slice the mushrooms when cool, and add to the shallots.

Deglaze the pan with the Marsala, and reduce slightly. Remove the mushrooms from the pan, and strain the veloute (slightly thickened chicken stock) into the pan. Simmer the sauce for 5 minutes. The sauce should still be very thin. Place the chicken, either whole, or sliced, in a baking pan, neatly. Cover with the mushrooms, and pour the sauce over the chicken. Garnish with sliced scallions or chives. The thin sauce will be soaked up by the overcooked chicken. Cover, and keep over 140 degrees for service.

This may also be made yesterday, and reheated in the oven pan for tomorrow.

CHAPTER 12

Writing Recipes

In order to define a dish, you need to write a recipe. A dish is not finished until it can be communicated completely to the next cook. Writing a good recipe is difficult. It has to be simple enough to be understood, but complex enough to bring your small methods through to the reader. It is those small methods that make good food great.

Understanding your reader is very important. You write a recipe differently for a novice cook than for an experienced coworker. For the novice, only the simplest recipes are worth writing, as every single step needs to be explained. Some of these steps can take a full paragraph and make for a very, very long boring recipe.

We like to write recipes in a style we call "cook to cook." We assume you know a lot about cooking and we don't have to explain much at all. This saves a lot of time and words, and allows us to write a complex recipe that will be easily understood and not boring. Simple methods like "mark your steaks" or "sweat the mirepoix without browning" would take paragraphs to explain to the novice but are specific to the professional.

Collecting Recipes

When we get a recipe from an experienced cook, we use the same style. If we ask a good cook for a recipe—say for a newspaper article—we are generally blocked by the cook's inexperience with writing recipes. The usual line is, "I don't have it written down. I have it up here." This is accompanied by a tap on the head. That doesn't do me much good, though. Doesn't do their grandkids much good either.

So we say to our prospect, "Pretend I'm going to make the dish right now. I'm a new cook on your line. Tell me how to make it." We write quickly, and when done, we ask the pertinent questions that make a professional difference. "Do you season the flour?" "Do you brown the chicken?" "Do you reduce the cream?"

Don't Sweat the Small Stuff

In writing a recipe, most people get hung up on pieces that really make no difference. They agonize over whether it's a quarter teaspoon or a half tablespoon of salt, when they could just say "Season lightly." They can't decide on the exact oven temperature for the roast, when "Put in a very hot oven and immediately reduce the heat to about 200 degrees" will do. It is not necessary to time everything to the minute. "Bake until it is done" is plenty specific. You are speaking to a cook, not a chemist.

Sweat the Really Small Stuff

What you do want to pay obsessive attention to are the parts that turn an ordinary okay meal into a great dish. There are subtle little actions and flavorings that change a dish from good to great. Most cooks don't think of those little nuances. What you do naturally when you make a soup or sauce is hard to define on paper, but it is absolutely necessary if you are going to communicate a great dish to the reader.

Such actions as "sweat the mirepoix," "deglaze the pan," "deep poach," or "shallow poach" may be very small, and their importance may not be recognized by the novice. An experienced cook looking for greatness, however, will recognize that these small actions make all the difference.

Seared Pork Tenderloin with Maple Peppercorn Glaze

The best way to set up a large dinner is to do all the work ahead of time. That's just how it's done in a restaurant, prep work is the key.

This dish may be set up so that it is a quick 10 minute cooking job to serve tomorrow. Or, you may set this up on Thursday, store the pork in the sauce, covered in the cooler. Slice it sometime Saturday, and put in the oven to reheat for an easy fine tasting dish that will impress your friends and amaze your enemies.

Makes about 6 servings

Pork Tenderloins	3 each
A lot	Whole Black Peppercorns
2 ounces	Fresh Rosemary
4 ounces	Pure Maple Syrup
3 each	Pork Tenderloins
12 ounces	Demi-Glace (or a high quality canned brown beef gravy)

Crack the peppercorns on a heavy cutting board, with a heavy sauce pan. Dredge the pork tenderloins in the peppercorns, covering all surfaces, as much as you'd like or not like.

Rub the tenderloins with a very little pure maple syrup and a little chopped fresh rosemary. Cover and allow to sit a few hours or overnight.

Take an oven proof shallow fry pan, like a cast iron pan, and heat on the stove until it's real hot. Add just a little oil, and put the tenderloins in the pan. Turn them over once or twice so they will brown all over, and then put in a 350 degree. Cover loosely with foil, and roast until just barely done. 130 degrees if you have a thermometer, they will increase temperature after you pull them from the oven.

Remove the tenderloin from the pan, and deglaze the pan with a little stock or water. Add an ounce of maple syrup, and the demi-glace or good brown gravy. Bring to a good boil, and correct the consistency of the sauce. Not too thick. Slice the tenderloin, not too thin, and arrange over mashed potatoes, or pasta or rice. Drizzle with sauce, and add a sprig of fresh rosemary.

Roasted Butternut Squash Mac & Cheese

This is a kid-approved recipe. Elementary students are hard to please. The color is very similar to regular old boxed Mac and Cheese, and it's a good way to add yellow vegetables to children's diets. makes 24 kid sized servings

2 pounds	Peeled Butternut Squash
1 stick	Unsalted AA Butter
½ cup	All Purpose Flour
½ gallon	Skim Milk
1 pound	NY White Cheddar
4 pounds	Whole Grain Elbow Macaroni

Cut the butternut squash into large pieces, and roast in a hot oven until they are getting soft. Do not allow them to become brown. Kids don't like brown. Mash with a mixer, or a hand potato masher when cool.

Make a sauce by mixing butter and flour, adding milk, and bringing up to a rolling simmer. Allow to cool to under 120 degrees, and add the grated cheese. Stir well to eliminate lumps.

Add the mashed butternut squash, and stir well to eliminate any more lumps.

Cook the elbow macaroni until just done, and cool. Mix the cheese and butternut squash sauce, and the macaroni. Place in a sprayed hotel pan, and bake at 325 degrees convection oven for about 20 minutes, until it is well heated, at least 150 degrees throughout. It should be bubbling, and only slightly browned.

Serve immediately, or keep in a steam table, covered, at over 140 degrees. This dish may just as well be done with yams or sweet potatoes, as with butternut squash.

CHAPTER 13

The Most Difficult of Great Food:
French Onion Soup and the Turkey Club

In my humble opinion, French onion soup and a turkey club sandwich are the two most difficult dishes to make great. You can order onion soup or a turkey club in every little restaurant and diner. Most everyone will order these two dishes and think nothing of it. We expect little, and that is what we get. A bland, insipid onion soup with some sort of cheese on it or a soggy salty turkey sandwich is enough to fill us up and keep us going for the rest of the day. But it's not enough to entice our culinary senses.

Take the turkey club. Done perfectly, this is a very complex dish that combines qualities of crisp, soft, hot, cold, salty, and sweet. Start with hot crispy toast with a little cold mayonnaise, add cold great-tasting roast turkey and crisp hot salty bacon, and top with crisp cold lettuce and sweet, soft, delicious tomatoes. Bring it right out to the customer, and it is a culinary delight. Let it stand under a heat lamp for two minutes, and it is all the same texture, temperature, and flavor.

As for onion soup, merely stewing some onions; adding some sort of broth or base and some fake soup base or additive; slapping on some toast points; and browning a slice of tasteless cheese will give the resemblance of French onion soup, but it is blah, bland, and in need of salt. Take that same recipe, use the Maillard reaction, keep an eye on umami ingredients, and cook it perfectly, and this can be just about the best thing you've ever eaten in your life.

Both of these dishes require concentration on umami and Maillard, as well as diligence in preparation and service. The turkey club needs good ingredients, such as high-quality fresh roast turkey, the best crisp fresh bacon, and good sweet tomatoes. The sandwich needs to be put in front of the customer right away after being prepared and plated. Then it has all the nuances and fine points that make it a great meal.

A side note: Good tomatoes may be found year round. It is not so much the closeness to the garden and time of year that makes for a good tomato, it is the storage. You buy a box of 5 x 6 tomatoes, and the receiver naturally puts them in the cooler at 38 degrees. This turns all the sugar in those ripe tomatoes to starch, and they taste almost as good as red sawdust. Take those same tomatoes and store them closer to 58 degrees, and they will keep their flavor for several days. You can ruin the best August Jersey beefsteaks by storing them in the refrigerator.

Good Onion Soup

Makes about 24 servings

2 pounds	Sliced Onions
1 Tbs	Vegetable Oil
1 Can	Chicken Broth 46 oz
8 oz.	Onion Soup Base
1 quart	Water
1 Tbs	Salt
48 slices	French or Italian Bread
16 slices	Mozzarella Cheese

In a heavy pan, heat the onions until they are well cooked, and starting to brown. Add the broth, base, salt and water, and bring to a boil. Put in the steam table for service.

When the soup is ordered, fill an onion soup crock with soup, top with two slices of bread, and drape with a slice of Mozzarella. Put under a broiler or Salamander and brown. Serve immediately

Great Onion Soup

Makes about 12 servings

French Onion Soup is the epitome of a dish which features Umami ingredients, and the Maillard Reaction as flavor enhancers. It can be either a pretty good soup, or just about the best dish you've ever had in your life. This is a soup which may be personalized, but it cannot be overly involved. Too many ingredient changes, and you do not have French Onion Soup.

4 each	Spanish Onions, peeled and sliced thin
8 oz.	Shallots, very small ones, peeled and sliced thin
1 Tbs	Olive Oil
2 ounces	Sherry wine
2 pints	Good Rich Beef Broth
2 pints	Light Chicken Broth
1 tsp	Worcestershire Sauce
1 tsp	Tomato puree
24 slices	French or Italian Bread
1 pounds	Swiss Cheese, shredded, preferably Gruyere or Emmentaler
4 ounces	Very good Parmesan Cheese, shredded

In a heavy pan, heat the onions at medium to high heat until they are completely browned. (Maillard) This will take a long time. Like an hour or more. The longer the better. They need to be stirred every few minutes. When they have developed a deep brown, add the shallots and turn up the heat, getting some extra color.

Let the pan cool, and add the wine. Raise the heat and deglaze the pan. Add the broths, bring to a boil. Keep the heat on one side of the pot, and skim the surface on the other side of the pan.

Add just a little Worcestershire Sauce (English Umami) and tomato, and bring to a boil. Put into stainless steel, cool, and refrigerate. Reheat tomorrow, or up to 4 days from now, to a boil, and keep hot in a steam table.

Slice the crusty (Maillard) French bread very thin, as thin as a pencil. Don't toast, but allow to dry for at least 3 days, so it is not just crispy, but will crack if handled almost at all.

Make a very thin layer of bread on top of the soup, in a crock. Sprinkle with the Swiss and Parmesan mixture, not too much, keeping the cheese very even all around. Brown in a very hot broiler, until browned and bubbling, and serve right away.

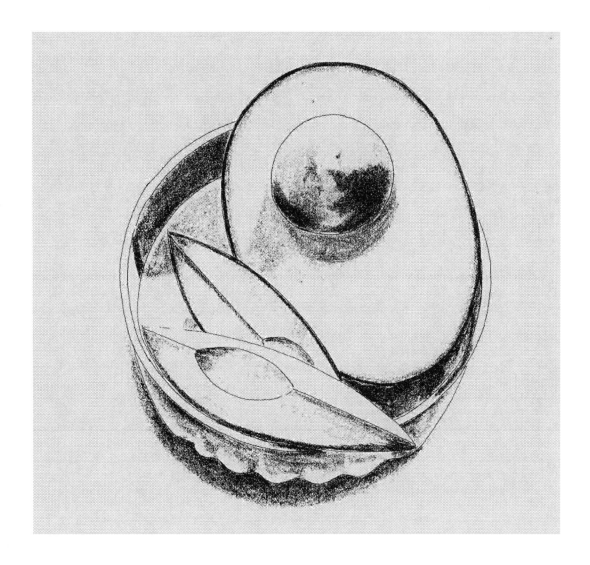

CHAPTER 14

Clean and Simple Food

For years at our house, we have been eating fresher and more simple foods. We grow a lot and freeze a lot, and the dishes we like best are those with the fewest and most simple ingredients. Great ingredients do not need salt, sugar, and fat to make them taste good. Great ingredients taste great by themselves, and even better in combination with other great ingredients.

Clean food has become a buzzword. It's even used by national chains in their advertising. At this point, it becomes just another term to use, like *all natural, applewood,* or *Angus*—words that sell well but do not really reflect what is actually in the food being served. Clean ingredients that are shipped across the country to be served are not what advocates of clean food are really looking for. Clean ingredients are simple, local, and free of agricultural and manufacturing steps that are detrimental to health.

The food we eat influences our weight, our health, our state of mind—all sorts of stuff. If we only listen to the giant companies who want to sell us stuff, we will only eat processed foods full of salt, sugar, and fat. As a result, we will develop all those wonderful health problems associated with salt, sugar, and fat.

If we keep our ingredient list simple, we will be healthier. It's as simple as that. As an added benefit, we will find that our taste buds are healthier. If there is less salt, sugar, and horrible fats passing over your taste buds, they will actually be able to taste! If you forgo salt for a pretty short time, like a few weeks, you'll be amazed at how you can taste small amounts of salt, and how little salt you actually will want to eat.

Fresh vegetables are clean food, but not the prewashed stuff that is probably weeks from the farm. Growing your own sure helps.

Good sugars are clean food. Maple syrup, honey, molasses, and such are actually full of nutrients, and are not just sweeteners. High fructose corn syrup, on the other hand, is just empty calories.

Minimally processed fats are clean food. If you look up the process used in making refined cooking oils, you will certainly avoid them. Heat, chemical additions, and genetically modified (GMO) ingredients are all part of the process, and it is closer to the petrochemical industry than a food industry, in my opinion. Cold-pressed oils from non-GMO seeds are good for you. XVOO and cold-pressed sunflower oils, for example, are great to keep on your shelf.

As an added bonus, I will give you these two recipes for house-made sodas. They are delicious and refreshing—with or without the addition of alcohol—and are good for you and your kids. The method is very simple, and you can use the same steps to make up your own secret blends. Just make the syrup using clean sweeteners.

Cole Slaw 2 Ways

makes about 2 quarts each, or 60 total side dish servings

It is difficult to find healthy vegetables to eat during the winter months. There are very good tasting lettuces and other greens, but they do come from very far away, and are many days, or weeks, from the ground in which they were grown. Many nutrients are lost over this time.

The vegetable ingredients in Cole Slaw, however, are storage crops that do not lose their vitamin and mineral content during those months they are stored. Cabbage in particular is a great source of Vitamin C, among other nutrients.

This method of making Cole Slaw results in a very fresh tasting, tangy product, sweetened not by sugar, but by the pickling of the cabbage, and by the onions and carrots involved. It is a very healthful dish. The two Cole Slaws served together are very unusual, good looking and delicious.

5 pounds	Green Cabbage
5 pounds	Red Cabbage
8 oz	Salt
2 pounds	Spanish Onions
2 pounds	Horse Carrots
1 quart	Good Red Wine Vinegar
1 pint	Mayonnaise

Carefully trim and core the two cabbages. Slice very thin with knife or machine, and keep separate. Salt the heck out of each bowl of cabbage, mixing the salt in very well to all the cabbage.

Peel and trim the carrots and onions. Put them through a chopper if you want, but it is better to grate the carrots if possible. Put the shredded carrots and chopped onions in one bowl, and just cover with really good vinegar. Press down the vegetables so they are all under the surface.

Let both these bowls sit for at least a half hour. Then mix the mayonnaise in with the vinegar and vegetable bowl. You can use a spoon, it mixes easily.

Pour out the liquid from the bottom of each of the cabbage bowls. Then cover the cabbage with water, and drain well. Do this again. This gets out a lot of bitterness from the cabbage, and wilts the cabbage so that it makes great Cole Slaw. It also removes almost all the salt, so that the Cole Slaw has great taste, but very little salt.

Divide the carrot and onion bowl, and the dressing, evenly between the red and green cabbage bowls. Mix well by hand, making sure that every shred of cabbage has some dressing on it. Put into food grade containers, cover, and allow to sit for at least 24 hours before using. Date the containers and use this product within a week.

Maple Smoked Duck

Makes 8 entrée servings, or 16 appetizer or salad servings

This is my favorite duck recipe in the world. It is a slow cook, long smoke that results in a very tender, crisp duck with magnificent flavor. It is great as a reheat or better as a cold dish, eaten right off the bone, or cut into a salad.

This duck dish has to be done outside, as it requires a lot of smoke over a long time, but it does not need special equipment. Any BBQ grill in which you can use charcoal will suffice. It does have to be big enough to separate the ducks.

2 each	Whole ducklings, 3.5 – 4# each
2 Tbs	Garlic powder
2 Tbs	Onion Powder
2 Tbs	Paprika
1 pint	Pure Maple Syrup

Clean and dry the ducks, including the neck and gizzards. Dust the ducklings with the spice mixture, and let sit in the cooler for a few hours. If you'd like, you may add some cayenne or other hot pepper to this rub. Then, coat the duck, inside and out, well with maple syrup by hand. Every nook and cranny, please. Replace the neck and guts into the duck, and allow to sit, covered, in the cooler for at least a few hours or overnight. About every hour, take the duck out, and pour the syrup from the bottom of the pan over the duck, making a good maple coating all over the bird.

Get a good charcoal heat going on a grill, and sprinkle with soaked apple or cherry wood chips. When the smoke has developed, place the duck on a cooking rack, away from the fire, and smoke at about 200 degrees for 4-6 hours.

Be careful of the temperature, and add enough wood chips to keep a good smoke.

There will be a lot of fat dripping from the duck over the course of the smoking time, so it is necessary to place the duck over a drip pan, or foil funnel, to be able to take away the fat. You don't want duck fat in the fire, as it'll make a fowl taste, and increase the heat too much.

When it's done, it may be eaten right away, or it is even better as a cold dish. Maple smoked duck make great salad, it can be reheated in a hot oven to crisp the skin, or used, sparingly, as an ingredient in soups, particularly lentil soup. This is not an acquired taste, most everyone will love this.

CHAPTER 15

House-Made Sodas

These beverages are examples of good clean food, simply prepared and easy to make. Surprise your guests with your own brand-new concoctions.

Raspberry Maple Ginger Ale

Makes about 1 quart of syrup, enough for 12 glasses
Ingredients

4 ounces fresh ginger
1 fresh lemon
1 pound fresh or frozen raspberries
8 ounces pure maple syrup
1 pint water
seltzer, for serving

Method
1. Peel and slice the ginger. Grate the peel from the lemon and squeeze out the juice.
2. Put the ginger, lemon juice, and lemon peel in a pot with the raspberries, maple syrup, and water. Bring to a boil. Cover and let sit on the stove for a half hour.
3. Bring to another boil and strain into another pot, pushing through as much of the raspberry stuff as you can. Boil this one more time.
4. Put in a squeeze bottle, and refrigerate. Use up within one week.

5. When you want a little soda, put four ounces of this raspberry syrup in a glass. (Using a squeeze bottle is easiest way.) Fill the glass with cold seltzer and garnish with a lemon slice.

Honey Cucumber Soda

It may sound strange, but this is the most popular of the house-made sodas we have used. For most house-made sodas, we use various fruit or berry concoctions with good sugars. This soda, however, gets a round of applause each time without them.

Makes about 1 quart of syrup, enough for 12 glasses

Ingredients

4 cucumbers, peeled, seeded, and sliced, plus extra cucumber slices for serving

1 ounce fresh mint leaves

1 ounce fresh basil leaves

12 ounces honey

24 ounces water

seltzer, for serving

Method

1. In a pot, combine the cucumbers, mint leaves, basil leaves, honey, and water. Bring to a boil, take off the heat, and let sit for a half hour. Reboil once and strain into another pot.
2. Put the syrup in the refrigerator until you want to make soda. Keep for up to one week.
3. To make the soda, put a couple ounces or so into a glass. Fill the glass with seltzer and garnish with a cucumber slice.

New York Maple Apple Puffs

makes 12 servings

New York apples are available all year long, especially for baking. This dish is easy to set up, and can be baked off in batches, making them fresh and fragrant all during the day.

It is important to understand the puff pastry baking process. You start with very high heat, which puffs the pastry very high, and browns the pastry, and then lower the heat considerably.

In this way the dough will bake through without burning, while allowing a very flaky crust to form.

2 each	Puff Pastry 10" x 15"
12 each	Macintosh Apples small
8 oz	Pure Maple Syrup
2 oz	Cinnamon
2 oz	Cabot AA Butter
48 oz	Ice Cream

Cut the puff pastry sheets into 6 squares each. Dampen the edges with water only, no egg wash.

Pare and core the apples, one for each piece of puff pastry. Make a small slice on the bottom of the apple so they will stand easily. Place the apples in a large bowl. Add the maple syrup and the cinnamon, and toss well.

Place one apple on each piece of pastry, and fill the center core with the remaining maple syrup mixture.

Dot the top of each center with a piece of butter.

Bring opposite points of the pastry together at the top of the apple, it should cover the apple without being stretched. You may have to trim the apples a bit so they fit the puff pastry.

Pinch together all the seams so that it forms a tight seal around the apple. You may leave the pastry plain for baking, or you may wash with a little bit of water, and sprinkle with some sugar. Does not use egg wash at all, or it will burn.

Place on pans with parchment paper, leaving plenty of room between each apple pastry. Bake at 450 degrees for 10 minutes, and reduce the heat to 300 degrees. Continue to bake for an additional 30 minutes, a total of 40 minutes.

Cool the pastries, and serve immediately. Or you may reheat for service.

Serve with ice cream, or whipped cream, with fruit or berries for garnish.

Maple Butter Blondies

It's not the Blondies which are the best here, it's the maple butter sauce. There are so many uses for this sauce that it is not worth listing them all. On top of ice cream, plain cake, muffins, you name it, this sauce is one of the best you will find.

makes about 24 servings

2 pounds	Unsalted AA Butter, softened
1 pound	Walnuts chopped coarse
2 pounds	All purpose flour
3 oz	Baking powder
1 1/2 oz	Baking soda
1/2 oz	Salt
2 pounds	Light Brown Sugar
9 each	Eggs AA Large
2 oz	Pure Vanilla Extract
18 oz	Chocolate Chips
2 cups	Pure Maple Syrup
8 oz	Unsalted (sweet) butter
2 cups	Heavy Cream
12 cups	Vanilla Ice Cream
8 oz	Walnut pieces

Preheat oven to 350 degrees. Place parchment paper on 2 half sheet pans, spray the sides.

Mix the flour, baking powder, baking soda and salt in a medium bowl, sift this mixture to make sure all ingredients are combined.

Beat the butter and brown sugar with a mixer on medium speed until fluffy. Beat in the eggs, one at a time, scraping down the bowl with a rubber spatula. Beat in the vanilla. Gradually beat in the dry ingredients until just combined. Fold in the chocolate and the chopped walnuts.

Spread the batter in the prepared pans and bake until they are light brown around the edges and spring back when pressed, about 35 minutes.

Meanwhile, make the topping. Place the maple syrup and butter in a small saucepan over medium heat and cook until the mixture bubbles and thickens, swirling the pan, about 6 minutes.

Add the cream and continue to cook until the mixture is the consistency of caramel.

When they have cooled, cut the Blondies into bars and serve topped with a scoop of vanilla ice cream, chopped walnuts, and a healthy drizzle of the maple-butter sauce

CHAPTER 16

Making Good Food Bad

Certain horrible ingredients are used indiscriminately in the culinary world, to the detriment of society. Most folks are so used to these artificial ingredients that they would not recognize the taste of real food. If a cook aspires to make great food, these "ingredients" need to be avoided at all times. They are not ingredients—they are chemical additives and do nothing but mask bad food.

I have been told by several fine European chefs that they must use these fake ingredients because "Americans do not have the nuances of taste necessary to appreciate the real thing, like we in [name a country]."

That is a false statement. The reason these fine chefs must use a fake ingredient is because they have not investigated the real thing and learned how to use it. Here are some quick examples of how to avoid any false flavorings and make food with clean, simple, and natural ingredients:

Fake Maple Syrup

You know this stuff. You know all the brand names. It is what everyone is used to and likes on pancakes—everyone who has not had a lot of real maple syrup, that is.

Fake maple syrup is simply corn syrup, color, and a chemical flavor. It is empty calories, and it does not taste good. Real maple syrup is the reduced water that flows from a maple tree in the springtime. It is delicious, and it has copious amounts of minerals, making it good for you too.

In order to use real maple syrup in most baking and cooking recipes, you have to concentrate the flavor. This means you just boil it down by, say, half. Be careful—it may boil over. And of course, this increases the cost of an already expensive ingredient. I did not say that great food is cheap.

Fake Vanilla

I have worked seminars where I put up some fine flavors, such as real maple syrup and real vanilla, and had people compare different types. Then I put in front of them the fake product. If you have ever enjoyed real vanilla in any dish, you would be appalled at the horrible flavor that is fake vanilla. Learn to use pure vanilla extract or dried vanilla beans, and you will be making much better food.

Truffle Oil

This is one of the great frauds perpetrated on poor schlubs by the gourmet food industry. They take cheap-ass oil, put in a few teeny tiny pieces of truffle, slap in some artificial truffle flavor, and sell it at a premium to unsuspecting boobs.

Using real truffles require a long process of learning and experimentation. Real truffles, either fresh or canned, have a very intense aroma that is an acquired taste. It cannot be duplicated in the chemical lab. And it ain't cheap.

Do not be fooled by that tiny piece of real truffle in the fake oil. It is just that: a tiny piece of something real in a fake product.

Peach Melba over Sticky Rice

Makes 12 portions

Helen Porter Mitchell was a very famous Australian opera star around the turn of the 20th century. World famous under her stage name, Nellie Melba. She became Dame Nellie Melba during the First World War for her fund raising for war charities.

In 1892, the great Auguste Escoffier created a dessert in her name, Peach Melba, featuring an ice swan, vanilla ice cream and peaches. In 1900 he created a new version, which we know well, with ice cream, peaches and raspberry sauce.

In his books, it is very simply defined, fresh peeled peaches, and seedless raspberry sauce. Escoffier made many variations, including ice cream, spun sugar, ice sculptures, but the theme stayed peaches and raspberries. This is our take on this great dessert, delicious, vegan and gluten free version.

4 pounds	Fresh Ripe Peaches
8 oz	Granulated Sugar
2 pounds	Fresh Raspberries
4 oz	Confectioner's Sugar
2 pounds	Jasmine Rice
8 cups	Water
8 oz	Sugar
2 x 15 oz cans	Coconut Milk

Scald and shock the peaches, by boiling for 10 seconds, and then putting in an ice bath, to make for an easy peel. Cut into slices, and sprinkle with sugar. Refrigerate.

Toss the Raspberries with powdered sugar, and allow to sit for a half hour. Strain through a china cap or strainer to remove seeds, to create Melba sauce. Much much better than any canned sauce you may be able to buy. Cover and refrigerate.

This recipe works with fresh fruit only for a month or so each year, like August, when peaches and raspberries are at their best. Any other time of year IQF fruit may be used, making a very acceptable dish.

Cook the Jasmine rice with water, and a pinch of salt, until it is almost done. Add a little sugar, and the coconut milk. Keep somewhat moist. Finish cooking and keep warm for service, or cool quickly to reheat. Serve the very cold peaches and raspberry sauce over a ball of very hot sticky rice.

Maple Gelato

This dish is a gift from us to you. This may be the best tasting maple dish ever. You won't like us when the maple is boiling all over your stove, but it's worth the effort

| 1 Quart | Pure NY Maple Syrup |
| 1 Quart | Heavy Cream |

In a large heavy sauce pan, reduce the maple syrup by two thirds, so that it is a very thick heavy syrup. Use a large sauce pan, as this will foam up if you don't watch it very carefully. I said, you have to watch it every minute for the 20 minutes you are cooking it, or it will end up on the stove, the floor, and on your shoes. Once it starts to boil and foam, it will not stop.

When the syrup is well reduced, take it off the heat, and allow it to cool just a little, to say 180 degrees, and pour in the heavy cream, whipping the whole time. Pour this into a shallow stainless steel container, and put in the freezer when it is at room temperature. That's it, that's the whole recipe.

This product has many uses. It can be scraped with a spoon for a delicious frozen gelato. It may be heated lightly for use like a ganache. It can be a flavoring to add an intense delicious maple flavor to cakes, cupcakes or any type of dessert. It can be used to fill in little Filo cup. And, it uses maple syrup.

CHAPTER 17

Reducing Salt Using Umami and Maillard

Reaching for the salt shaker at every meal is one of the worst dietary mistakes one can make. Even a little salt is bad for you, and most of the salt we need is available naturally through food products. Our taste buds get so used to the addition of salt that we think of a dish without that extra salt as tasteless. It takes weeks of no additional salt to open our minds to the world of the educated palate.

If a cook uses umami ingredients, the food will simply taste better. Making great food does not include the addition of just the right amount of salt. Making great food includes creating methods and recipes that will bring out the naturally available flavors, which are masked by salt.

If a cook understands the Maillard reaction and uses these techniques to bring out the flavor, color, and aroma that are naturally available in most foods, there will be no need for additional salt—unless your palate is either addicted to the stuff or so jaded by years of salt abuse that you can't taste anything but salt. Line cooks, who work in very hot conditions, actually need salt to replenish sweat, and so they use salt indiscriminately and to excess. This makes for really good bar food that'll sell a lot of beer, but it will not at all help toward making good food great.

There is also the "salt as a garnish" sect. These wonderful cooks will go out of their way to find the most beautiful, tasteful, colorful, rare, and exotic salts to sprinkle in large quantities over their fine creations. Say you've just made wonderful freshly picked local organic asparagus, steamed perfectly and grilled slightly with some of the world's finest cold-pressed oil. Asparagus is a naturally salty food, just like celery and tomatoes. It don't need no stinkin' salt. Now you sprinkle on some Pink Maui Wowie sea salt, and all this fine organic local produce tastes like is salt. It's good food made bad.

Here's an experiment: Do not add salt to your own personal food for a few weeks. Don't use a salt shaker for twenty-one days. You will feel withdrawal symptoms, but they will be mental, not physical. You will be craving salt that you don't need. At the end of three weeks, your taste buds will be renewed, and you will experience a world of flavor you haven't known in years.

If you are cooking in a health care facility; if you have been told by your doctor to avoid salt; or if you have high blood pressure, you need to reduce drastically and then learn to avoid the addition of salt to recipes. This is a quality of life issue. Notice that none of the recipes in this book contain the phrase "season to taste." There is no need. If you make great food, adding salt will only turn it into salty food.

If you want good-tasting food, use umami and Maillard instead of salt.

Peanut Butter Cookies

Makes about 200 cookies

This recipe is a basic cookie recipe which may be altered to fit your needs. In this case it makes a fine healthy cookie, with ingredients that are simple and pretty tasteless on your shelf, but become delicious and smell great due to the Maillard Reaction.

The method described is a professional method of making, rolling and freezing cookie dough which sounds cumbersome, but results in easy to use dough that can be baked in small quantities, at any time, with no notice. Your little toaster oven could be the home of 6 cookies in 10 minutes, fresh and hot.

Brown Sugar	1 pounds
Granulated Sugar	1 pounds
Butter	1 pounds (room temperature)
Eggs	2 each
Peanut Butter	1 pounds
Flour, H & R	3 pounds
Baking Soda	4 tsp

Beat the sugars and butter in a small mixer until creamy, like a minute on medium speed. Mix the eggs in a separate bowl, and add gradually to the sugar mixture.

Mix the peanut butter into the sugar mixture. In a separate bowl, sift together the dry ingredients, so there will be no little lumps of baking soda, and then fold into the sugar mix.

Divide the dough into parchment or wax paper, like one pound or more per paper. Roll gently so it is a long log, and roll up in the paper. This now goes in your freezer. Label and date it first.

When you want some fresh cookies, take out one of the rolls, and unwrap your dough. It may easily be cut even frozen with any kitchen knife. Cut into half inch sections or larger. Place on a baking sheet, either with parchment paper, or lightly oiled, with at least one inch between each cookie. Best if they do not touch when they bake and spread. Bake at 350 degrees for about 10 minutes, or until slightly brown.

Homemade Granola

Makes about 4 pounds of cereal

This recipe is perfect for large families, anyone with a bunch of kids to feed, or a restaurant with a good morning business. Granola may be used as a cereal or snack, and may be served in a bowl, a bag, or from a bin with a scoop. The ingredients are very fluid. The oats are the base, anything else you use is your choice. The third time you make granola you probably will be making a recipe that is uniquely yours, and will impress anyone who tries.

Oats	6 cups
Almonds, whole or sliced	3 cups
Sesame seeds	2 cups
Pumpkin seeds	2 cups
Wheat germ	2 cups
Extra Virgin Sunflower Oil	1 1/2 cups
Honey	1 1/2 cups
Raisins	2 cups

Pre heat the oven to 325 degrees. In a very large mixing bowl, blend all of the ingredients well, except for the raisins. Place the mixture in a few shallow baking pans, with enough room to stir the product. Bake for about 40 minutes, until well browned. Stir the mixture well about every 10 minutes, getting all of the crumbs off the bottom, so they will not burn, and so that it all will bake evenly.

Do not leave this pan alone. You will forget about it, and the edges will burn and ruin the granola. Check it every 5 minutes, and don't leave the kitchen until it is out of the oven. Call this "Granola Discipline". It is a useful habit in most baking applications.

It is important to make sure your ingredients are high quality, and fresh. Some old oats that have been sitting on your shelf for six months, or some low quality oil that's been around too long will result in a very mediocre granola at best, with a stale taste. Nice fresh oats, oils and nuts will easily make the best granola you've ever had.

After cooling the granola, mix in the raisins. The raisins may be totally or partially substituted with dried currants, cranberries, apricots, or any other dried fruit. Store in glass or plastic containers, or in plastic bags. Best if eaten within 2 weeks.

For your own signature recipe, change the honey to maple syrup, agave, sugar or any other sweetener. Change the nuts to whatever you want, almonds, peanuts, walnuts, pecans. Change the oil if you wish, although sunflower oil sure tastes good. Try a few versions before you find one you like.

Pumpkin Frangelico Cheesecake

This cheesecake recipe is the result of our having to make too many Amaretto cheesecakes. They are nice, but enough is enough, so we decided to create something new and exciting. Took several tries to have the flavors meld for the right combination, but it was well worth it. This is a delicious and unique cheesecake that is pretty easy to make for the average baking enthusiast.

makes 2 x 7" cheesecakes, or 16 slices total

Ginger Snaps, crushed	3 cups
Butter, melted	8 ounces
Sugar	4 ounces
Cream Cheese	24 ounces
Granulated Sugar	8 ounces
Fresh Eggs	5 each
Frangelico Liqueur	4 ounces
Pumpkin, canned	2 cups
Cinnamon	2 tsp
Ginger, ground	1 tsp
Cloves, ground	pinch
Hazelnuts	8 ounces

Spray the surfaces of 2 x 7" cake pans. Cut a piece of parchment paper to fit the bottom of the pan. Mix the crushed cookies, butter, and the first sugar, and press this onto the paper.

In a mixer, with a paddle, blend the cream cheese, and the second sugar. Scrape down at least once and make very smooth. Add the eggs slowly, while beating, and then the Frangelico.

Add the pumpkin and the spices last, and mix well. Make sure to scrape the bowl to ensure a very smooth, even batter.

Pour the batter into each pan equally. Bake on sheet pans, or hotel pans, sitting in at least 1" of water, at 350 degrees, for about 1 hour, until they are set. Allow to cool in the water for at least 30 minutes, and then put in the refrigerator overnight.

Take 3 cake circles, 2 of which are 7" in diameter. Unmold the cheesecake by holding in very hot water, or by moving over an open flame, until they are loose from the pan. Turn upside down, carefully, onto a larger cake circle, remove the paper, and invert onto a 7 or 8" cake circle.

Toast the hazelnuts (or other nuts), and grind them coarsely. Press onto the sides of the cake as a garnish. Cover loosely, and refrigerate, or freeze. To slice, use nylon fishing line or a long thin knife heated under running hot water.

THE FINAL WORD

There is good food. Lots of good food. Great food? There ain't much great food around. There are distinct reasons why some food is only just good and some food is just plain great. Umami and the Maillard reaction are two reasons why a dish will make the leap from good to great.

We want to make great food—a lot, all the time, for our family, for that dinner party of six, and for the banquet of five hundred guests. We want people to line up and ask for more. We want people to cheer and get hungry when they hear our names. That is great food. If we look into our techniques and our ingredients and we learn our ratios and do the dishes we know best, we can make great food a lot.

Making great food is not for the faint of heart. It requires dedication, preparation, experience, and knowledge. Most people who are new to the business and have only friends and family as critics tend to think of themselves as great chefs. They are not. They may be pretty good cooks—at least on one or two dishes—but they are not great chefs. Folks who watch TV chefs think it is easy. Plating is easy; great food has a lifelong learning curve.

Most of the better cooks we meet can make more than a couple of great dishes. But if you ask them what makes that dish great, they are hard-pressed to say exactly what they do that makes the difference between good and great. They just know that one dish is only okay and another dish is great. This one works, but that great one sells like, well, hotcakes.

Umami and the Maillard reaction are essential factors to understand if you want to know why some of your soups, sauces, and other dishes achieve greatness. Understanding these two items alone will help to enhance all your dishes.

We have all worked with great chefs. In our younger days, we thought we would meet many such artists—many people who consistently create great food. We did not. We met several and know about several more, but the world of great chefs is small. The world of people who think they are great chefs is vast, but most do not make the grade.

It is up to each of us to strive for greatness in each and every dish we make, each and every day. If we can do it once, maybe we can recreate it. If we can recreate it, and each time it's great, then we have a chance at one great dish.

It is for each of us to try to understand the reasons for that great background taste, that perfect texture—the color and aroma that make people hungry. Little nuances of flavor, technique, and ingredients make huge differences in the final product.

It is for each of us to try to make good food great.

ABOUT THE AUTHORS

John Griffin

John Griffin is a 1975 graduate of the Culinary Institute of America. He is president of the mid-Hudson chapter of the American Culinary Federation and is a certified executive chef and certified executive pastry chef with the ACF.

With his wife, Suzy, John runs a small organic farm in Red Hook, New York, along the Hudson River. They grow seasonal fruits and vegetables and produce honey and maple sugar.

Early in his career, John worked with three masters: Jean Morel in Hillsdale, New York; Rene Macary in Catskill; and Uwe Deising in Kingston. He opened Griffin's Bakery in Tivoli, New York.

JEFF GOLD

Jeff Gold has had a long and varied career, from executive chef at Lake Tahoe to his current law practice in Los Angeles. He is a graduate of the Culinary Institute of America, having also been schooled at Bard College and at Western State University Law School. Along with his law practice, Jeff teaches in the hospitality department at Orange Coast College in Costa Mesa, California.

Long ahead of the sustainability curve in his home life, Chef Gold has developed an unsurpassed cactus garden with hundreds of varieties, some towering thirty feet tall.

Jeff's long experience in exotic ingredients has been a major source of umami information over the years. Since he moved to Los Angeles with his wife, Bridget, the availability of Asian markets has rejuvenated his culinary repertoire.

Jeff has been on the forefront of taste combinations that predate commercial applications. He was using such simple dishes as honey mustard sauce, applewood smoke, and exotic grains long before they became culinary bywords.

His work also includes producing a very popular radio show, lecturing on culinary trends and systems, and judging culinary, barbecue, and rib contests.

ELLIOTT WENNET

As a commercial artist, Elliot created and developed a decorative arts production company catering to the needs of high-end residential and commercial designers and their clients.

Elliott has created and produced unique and extraordinary faux finishes, murals, trompe l'oeil, Italian, and Venetian plaster surfaces. He has also trained many future and practicing decorative artists throughout the years.

With his education, years of easel painting, and added practical years of working as a decorative artist, Elliott Wennet is now returning to his former artist career and love of painting. He says, "I am excited to be getting back to creating new works of art that come under the scrutiny of my personal vision and creative process. I have many years and experiences in the visual arts, and what comes out I hope will surprise and enamor the viewer."

From flying helicopters in Vietnam for the US Army to creating art for collections and museums, Elliot has won an international reputation as a serious and inventive artist. He has done stage and concert design and album cover work.

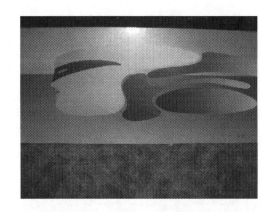

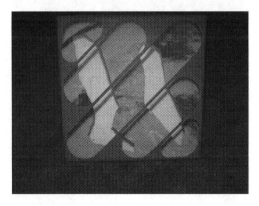

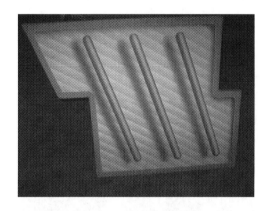

INDEX

bold denotes photo

A

A1 sauce, 72
Anadama Bread, 15–16
Argentinian Chimichurri Sauce, 34–35

B

Bacon Jam, 56
bacteria, 13
Beard, James, 15
Beard On Beard (Beard), 15
béarnaise sauce, 72
beef
    Cider Braised Pot Roast, 57–58
    Mushroom Beef and Barley Soup, 66–67
    Roast Brisket with Wild Mushroom Sauce,
        57–58
Biscochas, 17–18
Bordelaise sauce, 72
breads
    Anadama Bread, 15–16
    Challah, 19–20
    Irish Soda Bread, 27–28
"the browning effect," Maillard reaction as, xi, 23

C

caramelization, xi, 38, 52, 53–54
cereal, Homemade Granola, 120–121
Challah, 19–20

cheesecake, Pumpkin Frangelico Cheesecake,
    122–123
Chicken Marsala with Grilled Criminis, 78
chutney, 72
Cider Braised Pot Roast, 46–47
clean and simple food, 91–92
Cole Slaw 2 Ways, 95–96
Concasse, 8–9
cookies
    Biscochas, 17–18
    Maple Butter Blondies, 108–109
    Peanut Butter Cookies, 119
cooking oils, 92, 111
Corn and Avocado Relish, 42–43

D

"danger zone," 13
demi-glace, 72
desserts
    Indian Pudding, 26
    Maple Butter Blondies, 108–109
    Maple Gelato, 115, **116**
    Peach Melba over Sticky Rice, 113–114
    Pumpkin Frangelico Cheesecake, 122–123
duck, Maple Smoked Duck, 98–99

E

educated palate, 39
Eggplant Rolatini, 6–7
Escoffier, Auguste, 113–114

F

"the fifth taste," umami as, xi, 1, 36, 38, 59

fish, Lemon Maple Salmon, 68

flavorings, 70

flavors, concentration of, 23, 72

food safety, 13–14, 23

food-borne illness, 13

French onion soup, 24, 52, 84, 87

fresh ingredients, 23, 34, 42, 69, 70, 91, 120

fruit
    New York Maple Apple Puffs, 106–107
    Peach Melba over Sticky Rice, 113–114

G

genetically modified (GMO), 92

glutamates, 59–60

gluten-free
    Grilled Crimini and Asparagus Salad, 2–3
    Mushroom Beef and Barley Soup, 66
    Peach Melba over Sticky Rice, 113–114
    Roast Brisket with Wild Mushroom Sauce,
        57–58

good food
    defined, 1
    making good food bad, 110–111

Good Onion Soup, 86

granola, Homemade Granola, 120–121

great food
    basic great food ingredients, 69–70
    defined, 1, 63–64, 74
    making of, 64
    rules for making good food great, 23
    what goes into great food, 36–47

Great Onion Soup, 87–88

Grilled Crimini and Asparagus Salad, 2–3

Grilled Maple and Balsamic Glazed Pork Chops,
    44–45

H

hollandaise sauce, 72

Homemade Granola, 120–121

Honey Cucumber Soda, 103

I

Ikeda, Kikunae, 59

Indian Pudding, 26

ingredients
    basic great food ingredients, 69–70
    fresh ingredients, 23, 34, 42, 69, 70, 91, 120
    quality of, 23

Irish Soda Bread, 27–28

J

jam, Bacon Jam, 56

K

ketchup, as American umami, 72

kitchen cleanliness, 14

L

lamb, Rack of Lamb with Strawberry and Garlic
    Sauce, 10–11, **12**

Lemon Maple Salmon, 68

Liu, James, 25

M

Maillard, Louis Camille, 38, 52–53

Maillard reaction
    as "the browning effect," xi, 23
    caramelization vs., 53–54
    as concept key to turning good food into great
        food, xi, 125
    defined, 1, 36
    described, 52–54
    examples of, 26, 38
    importance of, 37
    a.k.a. Maillard effect, 52
    reducing salt using, 117–118
    use of, 63

Maple Butter Blondies, 108–109

Maple Gelato, 115, **116**

Maple Smoked Duck, 98–99

maple syrup
    fake maple syrup, 110

use of, 38, 54

meats
Cider Braised Pot Roast, 46–47
Grilled Maple and Balsamic Glazed Pork Chops,
44–45
Rack of Lamb with Strawberry and Garlic
Sauce, 10–11, **12**
Roast Brisket with Wild Mushroom Sauce,
57–58
Roast Pork Loin with Maple Water and
Mustard, 76, **77**
Seared Pork Tenderloin with Maple Peppercorn
Glaze, 82

Melba, Nellie, 113–114
Miso Soup, 25, **100**
Mitchell, Helen Porter, 113–114
monosodium glutamate (MSG), 59
muscle memory, 23, 37, 39
Mushroom Beef and Barley Soup, 66–67
mushrooms
Chicken Marsala with Grilled Criminis, 78
Grilled Crimini and Asparagus Salad, 2–3
Mushroom Beef and Barley Soup, 66–67
Penne with Roasted Tomatoes, Portabellas, and
Pesto, 32–33

N

New York Maple Apple Puffs, 106–107
non-enzymatic browning, 38

O

oils, 92, 111
organic products, 70, 117
Osaka Restaurants (New York), 25

P

pasta
Penne with Roasted Tomatoes, Portabellas, and
Pesto, 32–33
Roasted Butternut Squash Mac & Cheese, 83
pastry, New York Maple Apple Puffs, 106–107
Peach Melba over Sticky Rice, 113–114

Peanut Butter Cookies, 119
Penne with Roasted Tomatoes, Portabellas, and
Pesto, 32–33
plating, xi, 48, 49, 69, 125
pork
Grilled Maple and Balsamic Glazed Pork Chops,
44–45
Roast Pork Loin with Maple Water and
Mustard, 76, **77**
Seared Pork Tenderloin with Maple Peppercorn
Glaze, 82
pot roast, Cider Braised Pot Roast, 46–47
poultry
Chicken Marsala with Grilled Criminis, 78
Maple Smoked Duck, 98–99
presentation, importance of, 64
pudding, Indian Pudding, 26
Pumpkin Frangelico Cheesecake, 122–123

R

Rack of Lamb with Strawberry and Garlic Sauce,
10–11, **12**
Raspberry Maple Ginger Ale, 102–103
ratios, importance of, xii, 23, 36, 38, 74
recipes
collecting of, 79–80
importance of writing of, 37, 79–80
reductions
as deceiving, 72
importance of, 36–37, 38–39
relishes, Corn and Avocado Relish, 42–43
rice, Peach Melba over Sticky Rice, 113–114
Roast Brisket with Wild Mushroom Sauce, 57–58
Roast Pork Loin with Maple Water and Mustard, 76
Roasted Butternut Squash Mac & Cheese, 83
rubber chicken dinner, 48–49

S

salads
Cole Slaw 2 Ways, 95–96
Grilled Crimini and Asparagus Salad, 2–3
salmon, Lemon Maple Salmon, 68

salt, use of, xi, 117–118

sauces
 Argentinian Chimichurri Sauce, 34–35
 base for tomato sauces, 8–9
 Rack of Lamb with Strawberry and Garlic
  Sauce, 10–11, **12**
 Roast Brisket with Wild Mushroom Sauce,
  57–58
Seared Pork Tenderloin with Maple Peppercorn
 Glaze, 82
seaweed, Miso Soup, 25
sodas
 Honey Cucumber Soda, 103
 Raspberry Maple Ginger Ale, 102–103
sodium, effects of too much, 59
soups
 Good Onion Soup, 86
 Great Onion Soup, 87–88
 Miso Soup, 25, **100**
 Mushroom Beef and Barley Soup, 66–67
Stubb's BBQ sauce, 72

T

taste
 creation of new and interesting taste, 10, 38, 39,
  44, 54, 72, 78
 of great food, xi, 63, 64, 91, 126
 healthier taste buds, 91, 117, 118
 umami as, 60. *See also* "the fifth taste," umami as
 use of Maillard reaction to create, 52, 54
tomato sauces, base for, 8–9
tomatoes, storage of, 85
trisodium polyphosphate, 70
"truck to plate" cooking, 69
truffle oil, 111
turkey club sandwich, 24, 84

U

umami
 commercial examples of, 72
 as concept key to turning good food into great
  food, xi, 63, 125
defined, 1, 36, 38
described, 59–61
examples of ingredients, 6, 25, 60
as "the fifth taste," xi, 1, 36, 38, 59
importance of, 37
jokes, 60
reducing salt using, 117–118
use of, 23

V

vanilla, fake vanilla, 111
vegemite, as Australian umami, 72
vegetables. *See also* mushrooms
 Cole Slaw 2 Ways, 95–96
 Eggplant Rolatini, 6–7
 Roasted Butternut Squash Mac & Cheese, 83
viruses, 13

W

Worcestershire sauce, as British umami, 72

Printed in the United States
By Bookmasters